HISTORIAN'S HANDBOOK

A KEY TO THE STUDY AND WRITING OF HISTORY

WOOD GRAY The George Washington University

With the collaboration of

William Columbus Davis • Roderic Hollett Davison

Richard Catlin Haskett • Elmer Louis Kayser

Myron Law Koenig • Howard Maxwell Merriman

Ronald Bettes Thompson

HOUGHTON MIFFLIN COMPANY
BOSTON: The Riverside Press Cambridge

Quotations by permission of

Longmans, Green and Company for Mr. G. M. Trevelyan
Harcourt, Brace and Company for Mr. T. S. Eliot
Mrs. Eugene (Carlotta Monterey) O'Neill
AAUP Bulletin, Mr. William E. Britton, and Judge Learned Hand
The New Yorker and Mr. James Thurber
Charles M. Schulz and United Features Syndicate
Courtesy of *The Washington Post and Times Herald*

ABOUT THIS HANDBOOK

Many books discuss historical methodology. A considerable number of them are cited in the footnotes of the pages that follow. Among such works this *Handbook* is unique in the degree to which it is both comprehensive and concise. Its purpose is to introduce the college freshman and general reader to the nature of history, with suggestions as to how he may study it effectively; to guide the advanced student through the preparation of a term paper or thesis; and to offer the practicing historian a convenient reference manual.

This undertaking has benefited at many points from criticisms and suggestions from Douglass G. Adair of Claremont College, Thomas A. Bailey of Stanford University, Richard N. Current of the Woman's College of the University of North Carolina, Frank Freidel of Harvard University, William T. Hutchinson of the University of Chicago, Edward C. Kirkland of Bowdoin College, Leonard W. Labaree of Yale University, Arthur S. Link and Paul A. Schlipp of Northwestern University, Horace S. Merrill of the University of Maryland, Forrest C. Pogue of the George C. Marshall Research Foundation, Julius W. Pratt of the University of Buffalo, Carroll Quigley of Georgetown University, Wayne D. Rasmussen of the U. S. Department of Agriculture, Bennett H. Wall of the University of Kentucky, and Louis B. Wright of the Folger Shakespeare Library. Of the staff of the Library of Congress, Francisco Aguilera, Helen Field Conover, Johannes Dewton, John Hunt, Robert H. Land, Frank E. Louraine, Donald H. Mugridge, C. Percy Powell, Walter W. Ristow, and George A. Schwegmann, and of the National Archives, Katherine H. Davidson, W. Neil Franklin, Anne Harris Henry, and Leonard A. Rapport have all been particularly helpful. I am under special obligations to Guy Stanton Ford and Boyd C. Shafer, former and present editors of *The American Historical Review*. Additional suggestions and corrections for the improvement of the *Handbook* will be welcomed in the hope that it may ultimately be possible to establish a standard form of citations and usage best suited to the needs of historical scholarship everywhere.

The needs and wishes of students in some forty of my research seminar courses have provided guidance in the compression of the material contained in this *Handbook* into its present form. A number of these students, including Jean Rice Anderson, Dorothy Z. Brewer, Elizabeth A. Buser, Rachel MacIntyre Dach, Clarice R. Felder, Elisabeth B. Griffith, Thomas Page Johnson, Carol Patricia Koyen, Virginia L. Lee, Henry F. Beaumont Martin, Sandra Lee Myers, Eloise Randolph Page and Rosa D. Weiner suggested specific improvements on the basis of various preliminary drafts. All approved the concentrated and didactic form in which the work was finally cast — "a five hundred page book in sixty-four pages" — in which sentences must sometimes do the work of paragraphs and paragraphs that of chapters. They all united in urging all future students to read closely and to digest carefully, even at times virtually to memorize, what they read in order to derive the fullest possible benefit.

My colleagues whose names appear on the title page have at every stage provided suggestions, criticisms, and, in particular, aid in the compiling of bibliographies in fields unfamiliar to the author. The help given by William C. Davis, Howard Maxwell Merriman, and Ronald B. Thompson requires special acknowledgment. My colleagues John W. Brewer, Wolfgang H. Kraus, Hugh L. LeBlanc, and H. Rowland Ludden of the Department of Political Science, Philip H. Highfill of the Department of English, John F. Latimer of the Department of Classical Languages and Literatures, and Helen Bates Yakobson of the Department of Slavic Languages and Literatures have rendered special assistance. None of the above, however, are chargeable with any remaining shortcomings in either the conception or execution of this work, the responsibility for which is inescapably my own.

WOOD GRAY

WASHINGTON, D.C.

CONTENTS

v

Symbols Commonly Used in Proofreading Back Cover

AN INTRODUCTION TO THE NATURE OF HISTORY

> Time present and time past
> Are both perhaps present in time future,
> And time future contained in time past.
> > T. S. Eliot, Four Quartets, "Burnt Norton."

> Tyrone: Mary! For God's sake, forget the past!
> Mary: Why? How can I? The past is the present, isn't it? It's the future, too.
> We all try to lie out of that but life won't let us.
> > Eugene O'Neill, Long Day's Journey into Night,
> > Act II, scene 2.

History leads to understanding and wisdom. It is a road beset with pitfalls for the untutored and unwary, but the vistas expand as you journey upward and at the end a treasure house awaits if you have the necessary keys.

An early stumbling block may be the friend (or so you had thought him) who seeks to discourage you from devoting time to the study of history that you could be spending on purely "practical" subjects. This self-satisfied Mr. Know-All would probably have sufficient good sense to consult a properly trained expert about any such relatively simple matter as a lawsuit or business problem, a sick body or malfunctioning automobile, or a leaking roof; but he is likely to be in the habit of confidently appealing to the "lessons of history" as irrefutable proof for whatever point of view he may be advocating, without being qualified to pass a freshman examination in the field.[1] In the pages that follow you may find answers for him if he is not past saving.

You will also discover that, while it is comparatively easy to describe the methods of historical research, they may prove to be complex and obdurate when one begins to apply them to a specific investigation.

1. What is history? There are a number of interlocking definitions. Most commonly the word is used to mean one of the following or perhaps a combination of two, or all three, of them.

a. Happening. In one sense history is everything that has occurred, or has been thought, from the beginning of time through the last elapsed instant. Available data, however, are essentially limited to the period of three to five

---

1. The late Charles A. Beard once listed a number of facile clichés favored by editorialists and by the protagonists of various partisan and economic interests. (One might add to the ranks of habitual offenders military leaders, taxi drivers, and even, in their careless moments, professors and students.) See Charles A. Beard, "Grounds for a Reconsideration of Historiography" in Bulletin 54: Theory and Practice in Historical Study: A Report of the Committee on Historiography (New York: Social Science Research Council, 1946), p. 4. This entire bulletin of 188 pages, including a reading list on historiography and the philosophy of history selected by Ronald Bettes Thompson, will repay study.

billion years during which the physical universe has assumed its present form. Biological history may extend over the last third of that period, but its beginning is difficult to fix because the earliest forms of life lacked the structure that would enable them to leave fossilized remains. The human era, a brief one against this larger background but vast when measured against a single lifetime, may go back a million years or more. During most of his career man has been a savage who searched for food and shelter as nature provided them much in the manner of other animals. He rose to the level of barbarism when he learned to domesticate some of those animals and to cultivate plants. Only within the last one per cent of his existence has he discovered the civilized practices of specialization and the exchange of goods and services which have afforded him more and more time to devote to other things than mere subsistence. In this foreshortened span of time the rapidity of change has been greatly accelerated, and diverse civilizations have come into being and passed into limbo. During the past five hundred years world trade has served increasingly to make all men interdependent and to lead them in the direction of a single world civilization. In the last two hundred man has gone so far in unlocking the secrets of mechanics and natural energy that he seems to be speeding toward a crossroad where he will either go on to realize his age-old hopes or destroy every form of life on earth. His next step will depend largely on how well he has mastered the lessons of his past experience.[2]

b. Record. Only a small proportion of all the things that happen leaves any permanent record. At first glance history-as-happening may seem to dwarf utterly history-as-record, the only material which the student of history has to work with. Fortunately men have long made conscious efforts to preserve the evidence of what they have had reason to believe to be the most important occurrences not only of their own time but of antecedent periods. With his faithful co-workers, the archivist and the librarian, the historian spends much of his time searching for new evidence and making it freely available for study. Like the paleontologist who can reconstruct a skeleton from a few fragments, the trained historian can recreate much of past society from a relatively small number of clues. The evidence includes physical survivals, such as buildings and artifacts unearthed by archaeologists. About five thousand years ago, shortly before the building of the Egyptian pyramids, the growing complexity of economic and political activity in ancient Mesopotamia and Egypt led to the invention of writing. It is with the period since that date that the bulk of historical study, as it is normally defined, is concerned. The development of printing in the Western world some five hundred years ago greatly magnified the documentary record and the chances of its survival, serving in this respect to mark off the modern age from all that preceded it. In our own time photographic and phonographic

---

2. Every student of history should own George Gamow, *Biography of the Earth* (Mentor Books; New York: New American Library, c. 1941) , Rachel Louise Carson, *The Sea Around Us* (Mentor Books; New York: New American Library, c. 1951) , and Vere Gordon Childe, *What Happened in History* (New York: Pelican Books, Inc., c. 1946) — all inexpensive reprints — for an introduction to the beginning of the universe and man. See also Carleton Stevens Coon, *The Story of Man* . . . (New York: Alfred A. Knopf, Inc., 1954) , Weston LaBarre, *The Human Animal* (Chicago: University of Chicago Press, 1954) , Ralph Linton, *The Tree of Culture* (New York: Alfred A. Knopf, Inc., 1955) , and Norman John Berrill, *Man's Emerging Mind* . . . (New York: Dodd, Mead & Co., c. 1955) . Also in paper bound reprint.

devices have further increased the ease of record making, although telephonic communication has tended to eliminate certain types of written material that are valuable sources for earlier periods.

c. Field of study.   Out of all the varied types of records and remains preserved from the past, men have been able to piece together the outlines of their ancestral experience, fitting them into patterns of chronological sequence, location, and topical organization which offer us a better chance to understand ourselves and the world we live in.

Even primitive man sought to commemorate the experiences of his tribe in sagas and legends. At about the half-way point between the beginning of written records and the present time, Herodotus and Thucydides brought to history a spirit of truth and a deepened conception of the relationship between causes and results that raised the subject so far above earlier chronicles written merely to glorify some monarch or city that one might justifiably capitalize it as History. Both men wrote as exiles — which in a sense every historian must do in order to achieve the objectivity and breadth of vision that are demanded by the obligations of his calling. Following the decline of classical civilization, the mind of the Middle Ages was in some respects antithetical to the spirit of true history. The rationalist disposition of the 18th century Enlightenment once more directed men's attention to the need for comprehensive historical study. One of its fruits, after the cataclysmic quarter-century of the French Revolution and Napoleonic period, was the rise in Germany of "scientific" history as an academic discipline with full status. In 1825 at the University of Berlin Professor Leopold von Ranke began to inculcate systematic methods for the evaluation of documents, and set before his students the ideal of re-creating the past "wie es eigentlich gewesen ist" (as it actually happened) .

In the United States the study of history as a major part of higher education is a little over a century old. Earlier it was taught as a rather incidental subject — although for a decade after 1839 Jared Sparks occupied the newly established McLean chair of history at Harvard before assuming the presidency of that institution. In 1857 Andrew Dickson White, after graduate study in Germany (to which he would later return as our diplomatic representative) , became professor of history at the University of Michigan; and in 1881, after he had become president of Cornell, he set up for Moses Coit Tyler (who also laid the basis for the academic study of American literature) the first professorship of American history. White's successor at Michigan, Charles Kendall Adams, introduced in 1869 the German type of seminar course — the historian's equivalent of the scientist's laboratory course. Seminars soon appeared also at Johns Hopkins University under Herbert Baxter Adams, at Harvard under Henry Adams, under John W. Burgess at Columbia, and elsewhere. In 1892 a famous German professor, Hermann Eduard von Holst, came to the United States to be head of the department of history at the University of Chicago.[3]

---

3. Two discerning recent commentaries by leading European historians are Pieter Geyl, *Use and Abuse of History* (New Haven: Yale University Press, 1955) and Herbert Butterfield, *Man on His Past: The Study of the History of Historical Scholarship* (Cambridge: Cambridge University Press, 1955) . There have been a number of extended treatises by United States historians tracing the development of historiography. Most ambitious to date is James Westfall Thompson and Bernhard J. Holm, *A History of Historical Writing* (2 vols.; New York: Macmillan Co., 1942) . Briefer treatments are Matthew A. Fitzsimons, Alfred G. Pundt, and

In September, 1884, forty men (including Andrew D. White, Charles K. Adams, and Herbert B. Adams) met at Saratoga Springs to establish the American Historical Association. *The American Historical Review*, a quarterly covering every field of human history, began to appear in 1895. The first and long-time editor of the *AHR* was John Franklin Jameson, who also fathered the National Archives, the annual bibliography of *Writings on American History* (see page 27, paragraph 2-I-1-c below), and the *Dictionary of American Biography* (page 29, 2-I-6-a). By 1900 the AHA had grown to a membership of sixteen hundred. Now numbering over seven thousand, it serves to integrate the work of other historical societies in almost every section and state and in many counties and cities. The oldest of them, the Massachusetts Historical Society, dates from 1791. Altogether these societies publish over a hundred historical journals. They welcome students (for whom many of them offer special rates), school teachers, and the general public as members. Virtually all of the more than eighteen hundred institutions of higher education in the United States offer courses in history. Some departments of history have nearly fifty members on the teaching staff. Other nations have similar, if less elaborate, organizations and academic programs. There may be some ten to twelve thousand, or more, professional historians in the world apart from those teaching at the secondary school level, one-third to one-half of them in the United States.[4]

Even more impressive is the fact that the profession, particularly in the last generation and wherever its members are free from outside compulsion, has approached substantial agreement on major issues — while leaving each individual scholar entirely free to proffer new or modified interpretations derived from an objective re-examination of the evidence. Although prejudice, like fear in battle, is a natural human weakness, both can be brought under control by proper training and the realization that they will bring condemnation by one's fellows — an analogy in which intentional falsification would be equivalent to overt disloyalty. Exaggeration of the difficulty of achieving objectivity may be only an attempt to excuse oneself for not making the necessary effort. In the United States such once hotly argued subjects as the Civil War, international

---

Charles E. Nowell, eds., *The Development of Historiography* (Harrisburg, Pa.: Stackpole Co., c. 1954) and Harry Elmer Barnes, *A History of Historical Writing* (Norman: University of Oklahoma Press, 1937). Michael Kraus, *The Writing of American History* (Norman: University of Oklahoma Press, c. 1954), a revision of his *A History of American History* (New York: Farrar & Rinehart, Inc., c. 1937), traces developments in the United States from colonial times. William Thomas Hutchinson, ed., *The Marcus W. Jernegan Essays in American Historiography* and Bernadotte Everly Schmitt, ed., *Some Historians of Modern Europe* . . . (Chicago: Univeersity of Chicago Press, c. 1937 and c. 1942, respectively) are special studies of outstanding historical writers on both sides of the Atlantic.

4. J. F. Wellemeyer, Jr., "Survey of United States Historians, 1952, and a Forecast," *The American Historical Review*, LXI (Jan. 1956), 339-52, is a statistical summary from an exhaustive questionnaire that offers many interesting sidelights. Unfortunately we lack such statistics for the rest of the world. My comparison is based on scattered information and assumptions drawn from the fact that, as of about 1950-51, the United States could report 190,353 faculty members in all subjects (for 2,659,021 students in 1851 institutions of higher education) out of a world total of some 480,000 (for approximately 6,591,068 students in 7719 institutions). See Wood Gray, "Higher Education in the Nations of the World: Numbers of Institutions, Faculty, and Students," *AAUP Bulletin*, XLIII (Dec. 1957), 594-97.

relations, and reform movements have largely lost their power to divide; and closely knit "schools" or cliques of interpretation — characteristic of an immature stage in the development of any field of study — have largely disappeared. Exceptions to these generalizations serve only to buttress their over-all validity.

Among the many things still needed to bring about a more effective utilization of these advances in the historical profession are (1) the bridging of the chasm that unfortunately tends to divide secondary school teachers from college professors — except those of the "teachers' colleges," (2) the achievement of a greater appreciation of the nature and value of history by the general public, and (3) the encouragement of research in innumerable segments of the experience of the past that still await investigation. The American Historical Association is giving special attention to the first of these challenges by directing one of its major programs toward making new historical discoveries and interpretations more quickly available to the high school classroom.[5] The phenomenal success of such non-professional historical periodicals as *American Heritage* and the rapid spread of Civil War round tables and similar study groups offer substantial encouragement in regard to the second. This booklet is directed primarily to the third of these needs, but in a modest way it hopes to serve all three.

The achievements and needs of history as a field of study, however great, do not in themselves justify your devoting to it the time and effort necessary to attain some degree of proficiency. You still need to ask the question,

2. Why study history? Any of three possible responses should give you an adequate and reassuring answer. Together they should be irrefutable.

a. As literature. For at least twenty-four centuries written history has stood as a major literary form. Effectively presented, it has the ability to depict the unfolding of fateful events and to portray the rise or deterioration of character in a manner that ranks it with great novels and epic poetry. This function of history makes it incumbent on every historian, whether an experienced practitioner writing a book or the neophyte preparing a class paper, to cultivate a style worthy of his theme. Oral presentation carries comparable responsibilities.

b. As vicarious experience. All thinking is based, consciously or unconsciously, upon recollections of past experience. Man's unique ability to incorporate into his personal experience that of other men and women, not only of his own time but of all previous generations, is a true second sight that sets him above other species and enables him better to understand the present in order

---

5. Arthur Bestor, *The Restoration of Learning* . . . (New York: Alfred A. Knopf, 1955), a restatement of his earlier *Educational Wastelands*, sets forth some widespread criticisms of the disposition of departments and colleges of pedagogy to overemphasize teaching techniques and non-intellectual activities of pupils at the expense of subject matter. The AHA has issued to date, under the editorship of George Barr Carson, Jr., or has in press pamphlets summarizing recent interpretations of the Colonial Period in Latin America (by Charles Gibson), the American Revolution (Edmund S. Morgan), American Frontier (Ray A. Billington), Industrial Revolution (Eric E. Lampard), American Foreign Policy (Alexander DeConde), Jacksonian Democracy (Charles G. Sellers, Jr.), South in American History (Otis A. Singletary), Civil War and Reconstruction (Hal Bridges), and the Progressive Movement (by George E. Mowry). All of the above are obtainable from the American Historical Association, 400 A Street, S. E., Washington 3, D. C., $0.50 each. Of special bibliographical value, from the same source, is Margareta Faissler, *Key to the Past: History Books for Pre-College Readers*, $0.75. Ten or more copies of any one title of the above are $0.10 each.

to prepare himself to face the problems of the future. The philosopher George Santayana warned that "when experience is not retained, as among savages, infancy is perpetual. Those who cannot remember the past are condemned to repeat it." (*Reason in Common Sense,* "Flux and Constancy — Continuity Necessary to Progress.") And Woodrow Wilson declared (*Public Papers: College and State,* I, 255) , "The worst possible enemy to society is the man who . . . is cut loose in his standards of judgment from the past; and universities which train men to use their minds without carefully establishing the connection of their thought with that of the past, are instruments of social destruction." No two events in our lives or in the course of history are ever exactly alike, but recurring patterns of resemblance often make it possible for us to act with the confidence that comes from the recognition of the familiar. In the 19th and 20th centuries the heavy emphasis of the German army upon systematic and realistic studies of military history in its training programs was an important factor in enabling it to win great initial victories, while its opponents were having to relearn from their costly mistakes. In the end, the mystical self-delusions that were allowed to creep in and pervert German civilian history contributed to that nation's ultimate defeat and humiliation. An historian is not a daydreamer in an ivory tower. Only a person who is cognizant of the past can be a truly "practical" man, one able to free his mind from contemporary illusions and misconceptions and to select the path of safety and progress. He should also be a moral person, finding in the lessons of history pragmatic proofs of a Golden Rule pointing toward individual human rights and responsible democracy as the goal posts of civilization.

c. **As professional training.** Finally, the discipline of history offers training for useful and satisfying, although underpaid, employment.

(1) *Direct.* The teaching of history at both the advanced and secondary levels is entering a period of indefinite expansion as a result of increasing enrollments and of a steadily growing appreciation of the role of historical knowledge. In World War II the armed forces of the United States came at last to a realization of their needs in this field and began to sponsor the most extensive program of historical studies that the world has yet seen. Civilian agencies of the federal government have shown some signs of following this lead; and some state and local governments are already well advanced. Many business corporations are recognizing the continuing applicability of their past operational experience both by opening their records freely to independent researchers and by employing trained scholars without attempting to influence their conclusions.

(2) *Indirect.* Cognate fields and professions have long known that historical study was indispensable to their own proficiency, and this seems certain to increase as historians broaden their subject matter and continue to improve the quality of their offerings. One of the nation's greatest jurists, Judge Learned Hand, recently wrote to the president of the American Association of University Professors (*AAUP Bulletin,* Summer 1956, p. 264) ,

I think that the prime purpose of "higher education" is to establish the right habit of thinking, by which I mean thinking that holds its conclusions open to revision and is ready to consider any new evidence that is apparently reliable. That habit I believe is better acquired by a wide acquaintance with history, letters, and the arts than by specialized but limited disciplines. . . . The main thing is what will be the student's temper of approach to his problems when he gets through.

Without history the social sciences are like trees without roots, literature and the arts are flowering plants torn loose from the soil that nourished them, and philosophy runs the danger of becoming verbal gymnastics. The natural sciences, too, take on deeper implications and a broader outlook when coupled with history, both general and specialized.

3. How to study history. Systematic study is more effective and, in the end, takes less time than desultory reading and last minute "cramming." Some helpful suggestions are: (1) Prepare and follow conscientiously a planned schedule of two- or three-hour study periods throughout each week at regular times when you will be most alert and in an habitual place where you will be free of distractions. Colleges ordinarily expect at least two hours of study each week for each hour of semester credit. (2) Read over the assigned pages or chapter — if you are engaged in reading an entire book — rapidly in order to grasp the over-all theme and content. (3) Then re-read it more meticulously and, while doing so, (4) make a succinct outline in tabulated form of *not more than one page* for each assignment or chapter, which can be perused at a glance. (5) Down the margin of this outline make a check list of the more important names, events (with dates), terms, and other factual items included in the assignment or chapter. (6) Repeat this process for your notes on each lecture you attend. (7) Review your outlines and check lists at least once each week, being sure that you grasp the relationship between the facts and the larger patterns of interpretation suggested by your outlines. You need both sound structural materials and a good blueprint to build a satisfactory house. (8) Re-read those portions of your book or lecture notes which this review shows to have become vague in your memory or understanding. (9) Make out sample examination questions and, after answering them, revise your answers to make them clearer, better organized, more comprehensive and interpretative, and, at the same time, briefer and more to the point.[6]

There yet remains one further question:

4. Why study historical methodology? He who seeks to learn anything about the past will profit from a knowledge of the methods by which it is reconstructed for later use. It will be essential to him in one or both of the following ways:

a. Training. The preparation and presentation of a first-rate classroom report, term paper, or thesis can be a most satisfying experience. And, although to a beginner the prospect of seeing his writing in print is likely to be both exhilarating and a little frightening, the difficulties in the way of eventual publication in some form may not — if he has had the proper training — be so forbidding as they may at first seem. The topics awaiting your attention are endless in number, potentially fascinating to you and your readers, and varied

---

6. A detailed treatment is Clifford Thomas Morgan and James Deese, *How to Study* (New York: McGraw-Hill Book Co., 1957), 130 pp. Illus. $1.50.

enough to suit any inclination or taste. More than three hundred periodicals publish articles in the field of American history with some degree of frequency; and newspapers are receptive to interestingly written feature articles, especially in the rewarding field of local history. Where capable historians do not adequately fill such needs, other writers are likely to be drawn to fill the vacuum — with no small danger of spreading distorted and erroneous conceptions.[7]

b. Appreciation. Even though you may never publish a line, training in research methodology will be invaluable to you. Anyone who has learned something of the techniques by which a picture is painted or a musical score composed can have a greater appreciation of an art exhibit or concert than one who has not. In the same way, anyone can increase his appreciation of a work of history if he understands the manner in which its raw material has been mined and assayed. Furthermore, he will be equipped to check any questionable interpretations and to go more deeply into matters that particularly interest him.

In brief, research consists of six steps. You need (1) to select an appropriate topic, (2) to track down all relevant evidence, (3) to take notes upon it, (4) to evaluate critically the evidence you have collected, (5) to arrange it into a true and meaningful pattern, and finally, (6) to present it in a manner that will command interest and communicate to your readers the fullest possible understanding of the subject.[8]

---

7. Donald Dean Parker and Bertha E. Josephson, *Local History: How to Gather It, Write It, and Publish It* (New York: Social Science Research Council, 1944), xiv, 186 pp., with appendices and bibliographies, contains useful suggestions. D. J. Whitener, *Local History: How to Find and Write It* (Asheville: Western North Carolina Historical Association, 1955), 17 pp., relates primarily to one state but has general applicability.

8. Newcomers to the field will find Allan Nevins, *The Gateway to History* (New York: D. Appleton-Century Co., 1938) a stimulating introduction to history as a key to the comprehension of human affairs, which should be followed by Louis Reichenthal Gottschalk, *Understanding History* ... (New York: Alfred A. Knopf, 1950). Jacques Barzun and Henry F. Graff, *The Modern Researcher* (New York: Harcourt, Brace & Co., c. 1957) offers wise observations in a readable form. Carl G. Gustavson, *A Preface to History* (New York, etc.: McGraw-Hill Book Co., 1955) and Herbert Joseph Muller, *The Uses of the Past* (Mentor Books; New York: New American Library, c. 1952) relate their discussions of the nature of history to major periods of historical development. Fritz Richard Stern, ed., *The Varieties of History from Voltaire to the Present* (New York: Meridian Books, 1956) brings together evaluations of the discipline by leading historians. Richard H. Bauer, *The Study of History, with Helpful Suggestions for the Beginner* (Philadelphia: McKinley Publ. Co., c. 1948) is an excellent brief treatment in 36 pages, including bibliographies. Sherman Kent, *Writing History* (New York: F. S. Crofts & Co., 1941) offers much insight with a light touch. Samuel Eliot Morison, "Faith of a Historian," *The American Historical Review*, LVI (Jan. 1951), 261-75, contains the statement of basic precepts by a master practitioner. It is reprinted, with "History as a Literary Art" and other essays, in his *By Land and by Sea* ... (New York: Alfred A. Knopf, 1953). For the study of American history in particular, Homer Carey Hockett, *The Critical Method in Historical Research and Writing* (New York: Macmillan Co., 1955) is an enlarged revision of his *Introduction to Research in American History*, which has been a standard treatise since 1931.

1 | CHOICE OF A SUBJECT

> *Make no little plans; they have no magic to stir men's blood, and probably themselves will not be realized. Make big plans; aim high in hope and work, remembering that a noble, logical diagram once recorded will never die, but long after we are gone will be a living thing, asserting itself with ever growing insistency.*
>
> Daniel H. Burnham, Architect
> (biography by Charles Moore), II, 147.

> *The history of the world is the unfolding of human freedom.*
> Hegel, *Philosophy of History,* introduction.

In selecting a topic for research, you must first be certain that it meets *all four* of the following criteria:

1. Value. Your topic must be able to shed light on a significant, and in a sense universal, aspect of human experience — perhaps through your approaching it as a case study or by demonstrating its connection with some larger movement. Much depends on the treatment. The biography of an obscure person or the story of a small community takes on larger meaning when it is related to great events and evaluated as representative of far-reaching developments. On the other hand, genealogy and antiquarianism (the latter concerning itself solely with historical facts in themselves) are useful to the historian, but they are not history.

2. Originality. If your subject has been treated in some earlier investigation, you must be sure that you will be able to bring to it either (or both)

a. New evidence that is substantial and significant, or a

b. New interpretation of the evidence that is valid and demonstrable.

3. Practicality. Your undertaking must be trebly feasible in respect to:

a. Availability of sources to which you can have access without unreasonable inconvenience and with the assurance that you will be able to use them without the owner or repository attempting to censor your conclusions,

b. Your ability to make proper use of these sources through your previous background and training, including foreign languages and other technical prerequisites, and

c. Size. The scope of the topic you select must be suited to the medium in which you are presenting it (term paper, seminar report, article, thesis, dissertation, or book) and also to whatever deadline you may have to meet in the completion of your research. Most topics, however, can be expanded to take in a larger field or contracted to some constituent aspect after you have progressed sufficiently in your research to have a more accurate conception of the nature of your subject and the sources that bear upon it.

4. Unity. Every investigation must have a unifying theme, or be directed toward an integrating question or proposition, that offers you a point of departure, a direction of progression, and the promise of specific conclusions.

2

PURSUIT OF EVIDENCE

There was once a recipe for rabbit stew, so it is related, that began with the sensible admonition, "First, catch your rabbit." The following references should serve to put you on the trail. From the bibliographies and footnote citations you will find in these works, from further clues contained in the works they cite, and from persistent inquiry and correspondence you should be able in the end to compile a working bibliography of all the known sources of information. You may even have the exciting experience of uncovering previously overlooked sources.

A. General

1. Library catalogues. Your first step will be to consult the card catalogue of your best available library or libraries. The cards, now generally obtained from the Library of Congress in multiple copies, are customarily filed by (1) *author* (surname first, with authors of the same name listed in order of their date of birth), (2) *title* (by first word except "a," "an," or "the," or the equivalent in foreign languages), and (3) *subject,* under one or more headings, usually indicated at the bottom of the printed card. Keep in mind the fact that such prefixes as "de," "da," "van," and "von" are not generally considered a true part of the surname of Continentals; that Mc is listed as though Mac; that Hispanic people commonly retain the mother's family name following the surname; that the order of names among Asians often varies from Occidental practice; that there is no completely standardized form of transliteration between different alphabets; and that the German umlaut "ö" and Scandinavian "ø" are equated with "oe," ä with ae, and ü with ue in English. You should prepare a check list (which you will expand as your research proceeds) of key persons, places, periods, topics, and types of activities related to your subject and see what your library lists for each one.[9]

You can often arrange to obtain the use of other books that are not in your own library through various inter-library loan services about which your librarian will have information. Items held by the Library of Congress are listed, by author only (or, if anonymous, by first word of title), in

9. For the most efficient use of any library consult Frank H. McCloskey, *The Library* (New York: Reader's Digest, 1945), 16 pp.; Merrill Thomas Eaton and C. M. Louttit, *A Handbook of Library Usage for Schools and Colleges* (Boston, etc.: Houghton Mifflin Co., c. 1935), 43 pp.; Clara Beetle, *A. L. A. Cataloging Rules for Author and Title Entries* (2d ed.; Chicago: American Library Association, 1949), xxi, 265 pp.; Margaret Hutchins, Alice Sarah Johnson, and Margaret Stuart Williams, *Guide to the Use of Libraries: A Manual for College and University Students* (4th ed.; New York: H. W. Wilson Co., 1929), 245 pp.; *Ibid.* (abridged ed., rev.; 1936), 86 pp.; and Margaret Hutchins, *Introduction to Reference Work* (Chicago: American Library Association, 1944), xii, 214 pp., with bibliographical footnotes. For a broader approach see Jesse Hauk Shera, *Historians, Books, and Libraries: A Survey of Historical Scholarship in Relation to Library Resources, Organization, and Services* (Cleveland: Press of Western Reserve University, 1953), xvi, 126 pp.

a. *A Catalog of Books Represented by Library of Congress Printed Cards Issued* [from August 1898] *to July 31, 1942.* 167 vols.; Ann Arbor, Mich.: Edwards Bros., 1942-46, with a 42 volume *Supplement* through 1947, and continued as *The Library of Congress Author Catalog . . . 1948-1952* in 24 vols.; Ann Arbor: J. W. Edwards, Inc. About one thousand sets of the basic catalogue have been distributed to libraries throughout this country and abroad. Further continued by *Library of Congress Catalog . . . Books: Authors,* in annual volumes for 1953, 1954, and 1955, and *The National Union Catalog: A Cumulative Author List,* 1956, both published by the Library of Congress — continued monthly and cumulated quarterly and annually, with a five-year cumulation for the years 1953 through 1957 to be published in 1958. For listings by subject consult the *Library of Congress Catalog . . . Books: Subjects, 1950-1954.* 20 vols. Continued in annual volumes and monthly supplements, cumulated quarterly and annually. The Library of Congress also issues special catalogues of motion pictures and film strips and of music and phonorecords. A number of libraries also maintain a

b. *Union catalogue* on cards to facilitate inter-library lending. The largest of these, in the Library of Congress, covers some eight hundred American and foreign institutions. Entries from 1956 have been taken over by *The National Union Catalog: A Cumulative Author List* (see 2-1-a, above). There are about twenty other major ones, including those at Harvard and Brown universities, and in Philadelphia, Cleveland, Chicago, Nashville, Chapel Hill, Atlanta, Denver, Helena, and Seattle. Where it is not possible to borrow, you can often arrange by direct correspondence with the repository library to obtain microfilm or microcard copies at reasonable costs. See

c. Campion, Eleanor Este, *Union List of Microfilms.* Rev., enl., and cum. ed.; Ann Arbor, Mich.: J. W. Edwards, 1951. xvi pp., 1961 cols.; with *Supplement, 1949-1952.* Edward Bros., 1953. vi, 995 cols.; *Supplement, 1953-1955. Ibid.,* 1957. 1019 cols. The American Historical Association is preparing a Guide to Photocopied Materials of Historical Value in Repositories in the United States and Canada for publication in 1959.

Helpful also are the printed catalogues of foreign libraries, including

d. *Catalogue of Printed Books in the Library of the British Museum.* 95 vols.; London: William Clowes & Sons, Ltd., 1881-1900. With *Supplement.* 15 vols.; *Ibid.,* 1900-1905. (Lithoprint edition; 58 vols, and 10 vols.; Ann Arbor, Mich: J. W. Edwards, Inc., 1946, 1950.) New edition in progress; *General Catalogue of Printed Books.* London: William Clowes & Sons, 1931- . (Vol. 51 through DEZ, published 1954.)

e. *Subject Index of the Modern Works Added to the Library of the British Museum,* 1886- . London: British Museum, 1902- .

f. Wright, Charles Theodore Hagberg, and Christopher James Purnell, *Subject-Index of the London Library, St. James's Square.* Vol. I, to 1909; Vol. II, 1909-22; Vol. III, 1923-38; Vol. IV, 1938-53; London: Williams & Norgate, etc., 1909-55.

g. *Catalogue générale des livres imprimés de la Bibliothèque Nationale.* Paris: Imprimerie Nationale, 1897- . (Vol. 183, through TEDII, published 1955.) (Note that volume numbers running to three or more digits may be given in Arabic numerals.)

h. Preussische Staatsbibliothek, *Berliner Titeldrucke Fünfjahrs Katalog,* 1930-34. 8 vols.; Berlin: Staatsbibliothek, 1935.

i. *Gesamtkatalog der Preussischen Bibliotheken . . . .* Berlin: Preussische Druckerei-und Verlags-Aktiengesellschaft, 1931- . (Vol. 14, through BEETHORD-NUNG, published 1939.)

Learn the subject classification system of your library so that you will know where the works which you will need are shelved; obtain, if possible, a stack permit to scan the shelves; and run through the card catalogue or shelf list, arranged by classification call number, to find titles of books that may be charged out. Unfortunately, the major classification systems (Dewey Decimal, Library of Congress, and Cutter) were formulated at a time when the scope of history was thought of in a far too narrow fashion. As a result, a large proportion of books that properly belong under history are classified and shelved under other subjects.

2. Bibliographies.

a. Dutcher, George Matthew, *et al., A Guide to Historical Literature*. New York: Macmillan Co., 1931. xxviii, 1222 pp. Index. Work is under way, under the editorship of William Columbus Davis and the supervision of a committee of the American Historical Association headed by George Frederick Howe, to bring this basic volume up to date.

b. Franz, Günther, ed., *Bücherkunde zur Weltgeschichte* . . . . Munich: R. Oldenbourg, 1956. xxiv, 544 pp.

c. Coulter, Edith Margaret, and Melanie Gerstenfeld, *Historical Bibliographies: A Systematic and Annotated Guide*. Berkeley: University of California Press, 1935. ii, 206 pp.

d. Malclès, Louise Noëlle, *Les sources du travail bibliographique*. 2 vols.; Geneva: E. Droz, 1950-52.

e. *Jahresberichte der Geschichtswissenschaft* . . . . 1878-1913. 36 vols.; Berlin: E. S. Mittler & Sohn, etc., 1880-1916.

f. *International Bibliography of Historical Sciences*. Paris: International Committee of Historical Sciences, 1930- . This represents a resumption of the immediately preceding item. Annual.

g. Conover, Helen Field, *Current National Bibliographies*. Washington: Library of Congress, 1955. v, 132 pp.

h. Langer, William Leonard, and Hamilton Fish Armstrong, eds., for period covering 1919-32, Robert Gale Woolbert, ed., 1932-42, and Henry L. Roberts, ed., 1942-52, *Foreign Affairs Bibliography*. 3 vols.; New York: Harper & Bros. for Council on Foreign Relations, 1933-55.

i. *Bulletin of the Public Affairs Information Service*. New York: Public Affairs Information Service, 1915- . Published weekly, cumulated quarterly and annually.

j. Conover, Helen Field, *A Guide to Bibliographical Tools for Research in Foreign Affairs*. Washington: Library of Congress, 1956. iii, 145 pp. Index.

k. Conover, Helen Field, *Non-Self-Governing Areas, with Special Emphasis on Mandates and Trusteeships: A Selected List of References*. 2 vols.; Washington: Library of Congress, 1947.

l. Winchell, Constance Mabel, ed., *Guide to Reference Books*. 7th ed.; Chicago: American Library Association, c. 1951. xvii, 645 pp. Index. With supplements, c. 1954, 117 pp., and c. 1956, 134 pp. Formerly edited by Isadore G. Mudge.

m. *The American Historical Review*. Consult reviews of books and lists of articles in other periodicals in each quarterly issue of this magazine for items more recent than those covered by any of the above. Annual indexes included.

n. *List of Doctoral Dissertations in History Now in Progress at Universities in the United States*. Annual vols.; Washington: Carnegie Corporation, 1902-38. Approximately triennial vols.; Washington: American Historical Association, 1941- . Title varies.

o. *Doctoral Dissertations Accepted by American Universities, 1933-55*. New York: H. W. Wilson Co., 1934-56. Annual. Continued as part of next item.

p. *Dissertation Abstracts: A Guide to Dissertations and Monographs Available in Microfilm*. Ann Arbor, Mich.: University Microfilms, 1952- . Annual. A continuation of *Microfilm Abstracts: A Collection of Abstracts of Doctoral Dissertations and Monographs Available in Complete Form on Microfilm.* 1938-51. Subtitle varies.

q. *Paperbound Books in Print.* New York: R. R. Bowker Co., 1956- . Issued quarterly. Arranged by subject fields. *College Edition;* Spring, 1958- .

r. Brown, Everette Somerville, *Manual of Government Publications, United States and Foreign.* New York: Appleton-Century-Crofts, 1950. ix, 121 pp.

s. *External Research: A List of Studies Recently Completed* and *External Research: A List of Studies Currently in Progress.* Washington 25: Department of State, Office of Intelligence Research & Analysis, 1952- . Separate booklets cover some fourteen different areas. Also *International Politics,* monthly bibliography.

3. Periodical indexes.

a. Scott, Franklin D., and Elaine Teigler, *Guide to the American Historical Review, 1895-1945: A Subject-Classified Explanatory Bibliography of the Articles, Notes and Suggestions, and Documents,* The American Historical Association, *Annual Report for the Year 1944,* Vol. I, pt. 2. Washington: Government Printing Office, 1945. Pp. 65-292. Index. Supplement for 1945-55 in progress.

b. *Poole's Index to Periodical Literature, 1802-1881.* Rev. ed.; 2 vols.; Boston: Houghton Mifflin Co., 1891. With supplements for period from 1882 through 1906.

c. *Reader's Guide to Periodical Literature.* New York: H. W. Wilson Co., 1900- . Issued monthly, cumulated in annual volumes. Place of publication varies to 1913.

d. *International Index to Periodicals . . . .* New York: H. W. Wilson Co., 1907- . To 1920 issued under title of *Reader's Guide Supplement.*

e. *Annual Magazine Subject-Index.* 42 vols.; Boston: F. W. Faxson Co., etc., 1908-49.

f. *The Union List of Serials in Libraries of the United States and Canada.* 2d ed.; New York: H. W. Wilson Co., 1943. 3065 pp. Indicates location of between 115,000 and 120,000 periodicals in some 600 libraries. Supplements, 1941-43, etc.

g. Stewart, James D., Muriel E. Hammond, and Erwin Saenger, *British Union-Catalogue of Periodicals: A Record of the Periodicals of the World, from the Seventeenth Century to the Present Day, in British Libraries.* London: Butterworth Scientific Publications, New York: Academic Press, 1955- .

h. Caron, Pierre, and Marc Jaryc, *World List of Historical Periodicals.* Oxford: International Committee of Historical Sciences; New York: H. W. Wilson Co., 1939. xiv, 391 pp.

i. *Historical Abstracts, 1775-1945: A Quarterly Journal (in English) of Abstracts of Historical Articles Appearing Currently in Periodicals the World Over.* Eric H. Boehm, ed. 640 West 15th Street, New York 31. 1955- .

4. Newspaper indexes.

These gain additional value from the fact that an index for one newspaper often serves to guide you to the approximate date when the topic was likely to have been treated in other newspapers, either through a one time practice of widespread exchange among them or from the probability that they exhibited a simultaneous interest in the matter.

a. *Palmer's Index to "The Times" Newspaper,* 1790-1943. 601 vols.; London: Samuel Palmer, 1868-1943.

b. *The Official Index to The Times.* London: The Times, 1907- . Annual.

c. *The New York Times Index.* New York: New York Times Co., 1913- . Published monthly and cumulated quarterly through 1929, annually since that date.

Indexes for Sept. 1851 through Sept. 1858, for 1860, and 1863 through June 1905 are on microfilm obtainable from the Photographic Service Division, New York Public Library for $32.

d. *New York Daily Tribune Index.* 30 vols.; New York: Tribune Associates, [1876-1907].

e. Brigham, Clarence Saunders, *History and Bibliography of American Newspapers, 1690-1820.* 2 vols.; Worcester, Mass.: American Antiquarian Society, 1947. Includes location of files of these newspapers.

f. Gregory, Winifred, *American Newspapers, 1821-1936* . . . . New York: H. W. Wilson Co., 1937. xvi, 791 pp. Gives location of files. Includes Canada.

g. Brayer, Herbert O., "Preliminary Guide to Indexed Newspapers in the United States, 1850-1900," *The Mississippi Valley Historical Review,* XXXIII (Sept. 1946), 237-58.

h. Schwegmann, George A., Jr., *Newspapers on Microfilm: A Union Check List.* 3d ed.; Washington: Library of Congress, 1957. 202 pp.

5. Reference works and aids.

a. Langer, William Leonard, and Hans W. Gatzke, eds., *An Encyclopedia of World History, Ancient, Medieval, and Modern, Chronologically Arranged.* Rev. ed.; Boston: Houghton Mifflin Co., 1952. xi, 1243, lxxxix pp. Maps, geneal. tables.

b. Larned, Josephus Nelson, ed., *The New Larned History for Ready Reference* . . . . 12 vols.; Springfield, Mass.: C. A. Nichols Pub. Co., 1922-24. Illus., maps, bibl. XII, 10,773-10,855.

c. *Encyclopaedia Britannica* . . . . For many historical purposes the 9th ed.; 25 vols.; 1875-89, and the 11th ed.; 29 vols.; 1911, are more helpful than the latest, 14th ed.; 24 vols.; 1929 with subsequent "continuous revision." See also *The Century Dictionary and Cyclopedia* . . . . Rev. and enl. ed.; 12 vols.; New York: Century Co., c. 1911. Illus., maps, charts.

d. Seligman, Edwin Robert Anderson and Alvin Johnson, eds., *Encyclopaedia of the Social Sciences.* 15 vols.; New York: Macmillan Co., 1930-34.

e. Hastings, James, *et al.*, eds., *Encyclopaedia of Religion and Ethics.* 13 vols.; New York: Charles Scribner's Sons, 1908-26.

f. *The Statesman's Yearbook.* New York, etc: Macmillan Co., etc., 1864- .

g. Murray, James Augustus Henry, *et al.*, eds., *A New English Dictionary on Historical Principles.* 10 vols. in 13; Oxford: Clarendon Press, 1888-1928. Known generally as the "Oxford Dictionary."

h. Webster, Noah (original ed.), *New International Dictionary of the English Language.* 2d ed., unabridged; Springfield, Mass.: G. & C. Merriam Co., 1953. cxxxii, 3194 pp. Illus. Such dictionaries assist you to acquire a broader and more exact vocabulary and to discover the particular meaning which a word may have had in a given period.

i. *Webster's Biographical Dictionary* . . . . Springfield, Mass.: G. & C. Merriam Co., c. 1943, xxxvi, 1697 pp.

j. Barnhart, Clarence L., and William D. Halsey, eds., *The New Century Cyclopedia of Names.* 3 vols.; New York: Appleton-Century-Crofts, Inc., c. 1954.

k. Grimal, Pierre, *Dictionnaire des biographies.* 2 vols. in 1. Paris: Presses Universitaires de France, 1958. Plates.

l. Keller, Helen Rex, *The Dictionary of Dates.* 2 vols.; New York: Macmillan Co., 1934.

m. Bartlett, John, *Familiar Quotations* . . . . 13th ed.; Boston: Little, Brown & Co., c. 1955. xxxiv, 1614 pp.

n. *The Oxford Dictionary of Quotations.* 2d ed.; London, New York, etc.: Oxford University Press, 1953. xix, 1003 pp.

o. Mencken, Henry Louis, *A New Dictionary of Quotations on Historical Principles* . . . . New York: A. A. Knopf, c. 1942. xiii, 1347 pp.

6. Atlases and gazetteers.

a. Palmer, Robert R., *et al.*, *Atlas of World History.* Chicago: Rand, McNally & Co., 1957. 216 pp., 128 maps (92 colored). $5.00.

b. Fox, Edward W., and H. S. Deighton, *Atlas of European History.* New York: Oxford University Press, 1957. 64 maps, gazetteer, exercises. $3.95 (paper bound $3.65).

c. Shepherd, William Robert, *Historical Atlas.* 8th ed.; New York: Barnes & Noble, 1956. 226 pp. maps, 115 pp. index. $12.50.

d. Bartholomew, John George, *A Literary and Historical Atlas.* 4 vols.; London: J. M. Dent & Sons, Ltd., New York: E. P. Dutton & Co., 1913-36.

e. Muir, Ramsey, *Historical Atlas, Mediaeval and Modern.* 8th ed.; London: George Philip & Son, Ltd., 1956. xvi, 31 pp., 96 colored maps.

f. *Atlas zur Weltgeschichte* . . . . Berlin, etc.: Georg Westermann Verlag Braunschweig, 1956. vi, 160 pp.

g. Zeissig, Hans, *Neuer Geschichts-und Kulturatlas* . . . . Hamburg: Atlantik-Verlag, c. 1950. 10 pp., 138 colored maps.

h. Breasted, James Henry, Carl F. Huth, and Samuel Bannister Harding, *European History Atlas.* 10th ed.; Chicago: Denoyer-Geppert Co., c. 1954. lxx, 62 pp. Paper bound $1.75.

i. *Hammond's Historical Atlas.* Maplewood, N. J.: C. S. Hammond & Co., 1957. 48 pp. $0.50.

j. *Oxford Economic Atlas of the World.* Oxford: Oxford University, 1954. viii, 113, 152 pp.

k. Humlum, Johannes, *Atlas of Economic Geography.* 4th ed.; London: Meiklejohn & Son, Ltd., c. 1955. xii, 127 pp.

l. *Hammond's World Atlas For Students.* New York & Maplewood, N. J.: C. S. Hammond & Co., c. 1956. ii, 50 pp. $0.59.

m. *The Times Atlas.* 5 vols.; London: Times Publishing Co., Ltd., 1954- . Vol. III, *Northern Europe,* and IV, *Mediterranean and Africa,* published to date. Vol. I, *World, Australia, and East Asia,* II, *India, Middle East, and Russia,* and V, *The Americas* to follow.

n. Vidal de la Blache, Paul Marie Joseph, and L. Gallois, eds., *Géographie universelle.* 15 vols.; Paris: A. Colin, 1927-48.

o. *Rand McNally Cosmopolitan World Atlas.* New York, Chicago, & San Francisco: Rand McNally & Co., 1956. xxxii, 173 pp. Plates, index.

p. *Webster's Geographical Dictionary* . . . . Rev. ed.; Springfield, Mass.: G. & C. Merriam Co., c. 1949. xxxi, 1293 pp.

q. Seltzer, Leon E., ed., *The Columbia Lippincott Gazetteer of the World.* New York: Columbia University Press, Philadelphia: J. B. Lippincott Co., 1952, x, 2148 pp. New edition in progress.

B. Ancient

1. Bibliographical references.

a. Bury, John Bagnell, *et al.*, eds., *The Cambridge Ancient History.* 12 vols., 5 vols. of plates; Cambridge: Cambridge University Press, New York: Macmillan Co., 1923-39. Bibls. at ends of vols.

b. Glotz, Gustave, *et al.*, *Histoire générale.* 12 vols.; Paris: Presses Universitaires de France, 1925-47.

c. Swain, Joseph Ward, *The Ancient World*. 2 vols.; New York: Harper & Bros., c. 1950. Bibls. I, 553-68, II, 627-45.

2. Translated sources.

a. Smith, F. Seymour, *The Classics in Translation: An Annotated Guide* . . . . New York: Charles Scribner's Sons, 1930. 307 pp.

b. Loeb, James (founder), *Loeb Classical Library*. Cambridge, Mass.: Harvard University Press, 1912-   . About 400 vols.

3. Aids and atlases.

a. Woodcock, Percival George, *Concise Dictionary of Ancient History*. New York: Philosophical Library, c. 1955. 465 pp.

b. Whibley, Leonard, *A Companion to Greek Studies*. 4th ed.; Cambridge: Cambridge University Press, 1931. xxxviii, 790 pp. Illus., maps.

c. Sandys, John Edwin, *A Companion to Latin Studies*. 3d ed.; Cambridge: Cambridge University Press, 1925. xxxv, 891 pp. Illus., maps.

d. Pauly, August Friederick von, *Paulys Real-Encyclopädie der classischen Altertumswissenschaft*. Rev. by Georg Wissowa; Stuttgart: J. B. Metzler, 1894-   . About 34 vols. published.

e. *Oxford Classical Dictionary*. Oxford: Clarendon Press, 1949. xix, 971 pp. Incl. bibls.

f. *Atlas of Ancient and Classical Geography*. New ed.; Everyman's Library; London: J. M. Dent & Sons, Ltd., New York: E. P. Dutton & Co., c. 1933. xii, 268 pp.

C. Medieval

1. Guides and bibliographies.

a. Paetow, Louis John, *A Guide to the Study of Medieval History*. Rev. ed.; New York: F. S. Crofts & Co., 1931. xvii, 643 pp. Index.

b. Thompson, James Westfall, *Reference Studies in Medieval History*. 3d ed.; 3 vols.; Chicago: University of Chicago Press, c. 1925-30.

c. Williams, Harry Franklin, *An Index of Mediaeval Studies Published in Festschriften, 1865-1946* . . . . Berkeley: University of California Press, 1951. x, 165 pp.

d. Ricci, Seymour de, *Census of Medieval and Renaissance Manuscripts in the United States and Canada*. 3 vols.; New York: H. W. Wilson Co., 1935-40.

e. Case, Shirley Jackson, *et al.*, *A Bibliographical Guide to the History of Christianity*. Chicago: University of Chicago Press, c. 1931. xi, 265 pp.

f. Farrar, Clarissa Palmer, and Austin P. Evans, *Bibliography of English Translations from Medieval Sources*. New York: Columbia University Press, 1946. xiii, 534 pp.

g. Bonser, Wilfred, *An Anglo-Saxon and Celtic Bibliography, 450-1087, with Indices*. 2 vols.; Berkeley: University of California Press, Oxford: Basil Blackwell, 1957.

h. *Speculum* and *The American Historical Review* for recent book reviews and articles.

2. Bibliographical references.

a. Gwatkin, H. M., *et al.*, *Cambridge Medieval History*. 8 vols.; Cambridge: Cambridge University Press; New York: Macmillan Co., 1911-36. Planned by John Bagnell Bury.

b. LaMonte, John Life, *The World of the Middle Ages* . . . . New York: Appleton-Century-Crofts, c. 1949. Illus., maps, index. Bibl. pp. 766-82.

c. Clapham, John Harold, and Eileen Power, eds., *Cambridge Economic History of Europe* . . . . 2 vols. to date; Cambridge: Cambridge University Press, 1941- .

d. *Progress of Medieval and Renaissance Studies in the United States of America and Canada.* Boulder: University of Colorado Press, 1923- . Title varies.

e. Ferguson, Wallace Klippert, *The Renaissance in Historical Thought: Five Centuries of Interpretation.* Boston: Houghton Mifflin Co., c. 1948. xiii, 429 pp. Bibl. 398-407; bibl. footnotes.

3. Manuscripts.

a. Clark, Kenneth Willis, *Checklist of Manuscripts in the Libraries of the Greek and Armenian Patriarchates in Jerusalem Microfilmed for the Library of Congress, 1949-50* . . . . Washington: Library of Congress, 1953. 44 pp.

b. Clark, Kenneth Willis, *Checklist of Manuscripts in St. Catherine's Monastery, Mount Sinai Microfilmed for the Library of Congress, 1950* . . . . Washington: Library of Congress, 1952. 53 pp.

4. Aids.

a. Roeder, William S., *Dictionary of European History.* New York: Philosophical Library, 1954. viii, 316 pp.

b. East, William Gordon, *An Historical Geography of Europe.* 3d ed.; London: Methuen Co., c. 1948. xx, 480 pp.

D. Modern Europe

1. Bibliographies.

a. Bromley, John Selwyn, and A. Goodwin, *A Select List of Works on Europe and Europe Overseas, 1715-1815.* Oxford: Clarendon Press, 1956. xii, 132 pp.

b. Bullock, Alan Louis Charles, and Alan John Percivale Taylor, *A Select List of Books on European History, 1815-1914.* 2d ed.; Oxford: Clarendon Press, 1957. 79 pp.

c. Ragatz, Lowell Joseph, *A Bibliography for the Study of European History, 1815 to 1939.* Ann Arbor, Mich.: Edwards Bros., c. 1942, xiv, 272 pp. With three supplements: I, 1943, 74 pp.; II, 1945, 73 pp.; III, 1955, 154 pp.

d. Conover, Helen Field, *Introduction to Europe: A Selective Guide to Background Reading.* Washington: Library of Congress, 1950. 201 pp. *Supplement,* 1955. 181 pp.

e. Pinson, Koppel Shub, *A Bibliographical Introduction to Nationalism.* New York: Columbia University Press, 1935. 70 pp.

f. Deutsch, Karl Wolfgang, *Interdisciplinary Bibliography on Nationalism.* Cambridge, Mass.: Technology Press of Massachusetts Institute of Technology, 1956. 165 pp.

g. Hopper, Vincent Foster, and Bernard D. N. Grebanier, *Bibliography of European Literature.* Brooklyn: Barron's Educational Series, c. 1954. 158 pp.

h. Stieg, Louis F., *A Union List of Printed Collections of Source Materials on European History in New York State Libraries.* New York: New York Library Association, 1944. 112 pp.

i. Gregory, Winifred, *List of the Serial Publications of Foreign Governments, 1815-1931.* New York: H. W. Wilson Co., 1932. 720 pp.

j. Stewart, John Hall, *France, 1715-1815: A Guide to Materials in Cleveland* . . . . Cleveland: Western Reserve University Press, 1942. xxxiii, 522 pp.

k. Caron, Pierre, *Bibliographie des travaux publiés de 1866 à 1897 sur l'histoire* *de la France depuis 1789.* Paris: E. Cornély, 1907-12. xxxix, 831 pp. See author entry for later volumes.

l. Farmer, Paul, *France Reviews Its Revolutionary Origins: Social Politics and Historical Opinion in the Third Republic.* New York: Columbia University Press, 1944. vi, 145 pp.

m. Bithell, Jethro, ed., *Germany: A Companion to German Studies.* 5th ed., rev. and enl.; London: Methuen, c. 1955. xii, 578 pp.

n. Dahlmann, Friedrich Christoph, *Quellenkunde der deutschen Geschichte.* 2 vols.; Liepzig: K. F. Koehler, 1931-32. Often referred to as "Dahlmann-Waitz."

o. Pinson, Koppel Shub, *Modern Germany* . . . . New York: Macmillan Co., 1954. Bibl. notes, pp. 579-613.

p. *Jahresberichte für Deutsche Geschichte,* 1949- . Berlin: Deutsche Akademie der Wissenschaften Verlag, 1952- . Supplemented, for period from World War I, by *Vierteljahrshefte für Zeitgeschichte.* Stuttgart: Deutsche Verlags-Anstalt, 1953- .

q. *The Journal of Modern History* and *The American Historical Review* for recent book reviews and articles.

r. See also various catalogues of Stanford University Hoover Institute and Library . . . .

2. Bibliographical references.

a. *Histoire et historiens depuis cinquante ans* . . . *de 1876 à 1926* . . . . 2 vols.; Paris: F. Alcan, 1927-28. An introduction to historical studies by countries.

b. Ward, Adolphus William, *et al.,* eds., *The Cambridge Modern History.* 14 vols.; Cambridge: Cambridge University Press, 1902-06. Bibls. at end of vols. "Genealogical Tables and Lists," XIII, 1-205. *Atlas,* XIV.

c. Langer, William Leonard, ed., *The Rise of Modern Europe.* 20 vols.; New York: Harper & Bros., 1934- . (13 vols. published to 1956.)

d. Halphen, Louis, and Philippe Sagnac, eds., *Peuples et civilisations.* 20 vols.; Paris: F. Alcan, etc., 1926- .

e. Renouvin, Pierre, ed., *Histoire des relations internationales.* 7 vols.; Paris: Hachette, 1953- .

f. Taylor, Alan John Percivale, *The Struggle for Mastery in Europe, 1848-1918.* Oxford: Clarendon Press, 1954. See bibliographical essay, pp. 569-601.

g. Palmer, Robert Roswell, *A History of the Modern World.* New York: Alfred A. Knopf, 1950. Bibl. by Fredrick Aandahl, Jr., pp. 845-900.

h. Heaton, Herbert, *Economic History of Europe.* Rev. ed.; New York: Harper & Bros., c. 1948. xiv, 792 pp. Maps, charts, index.

3. Manuscripts.

a. Weinberg, Gerhard, and Fritz T. Epstein, *Guide to Captured German Documents.* Maxwell Air Force Base, Ala.: Air University Human Resources Research Institute, 1952, ix, 90 pp. Supplement in preparation. Microfilm copies of documents available from National Archives and Records Service, Washington 25, D. C.

4. Aids.

(See 2-C-4, above.)

E. British Commonwealth

1. Guides and bibliographies.

a. Gross, Charles, *The Sources and Literature of English History from the Earliest Times to about 1485.* 2d ed.; London & New York: Longmans, Green & Co., 1915.

xxiii, 820 pp. Index. The American Historical Association is making arrangements to have this volume and those of Read and Davies, following, brought up to date.

b. Read, Conyers, *Bibliography of British History, Tudor Period, 1485-1603.* Oxford: Clarendon Press, 1933. xxiii, 467 pp. Index.

c. Davies, Godfrey, *Bibliography of British History, Stuart Period, 1603-1714.* Oxford: Clarendon Press, 1928. x, 459 pp. Index.

d. Grose, Clyde Leclare, *A Select Bibliography of British History, 1660-1760.* Chicago: University of Chicago Press, c. 1939. xxv, 507 pp.

e. Morgan, William Thomas, *A Bibliography of British History (1700-1715)* . . . . 5 vols.; Bloomington: Indiana University Press, 1934-42.

f. Pargellis, Stanley McCrory, and D. J. Medley, *Bibliography of British History: The Eighteenth Century, 1714-1789.* Oxford: Clarendon Press, 1951. xxvi, 642 pp.

g. Williams, Judith Blow, *A Guide to the Printed Materials for English Social and Economic History, 1750-1850.* 2 vols.; New York: Columbia University Press, 1926.

h. Trotter, Reginald George, *Canadian History: A Syllabus and Guide to Reading.* New and enl. ed.; Toronto: Macmillan Co., Ltd., 1934. xiv, 193 pp.

i. Conover, Helen Field, *The British Empire in Africa: Selected References.* 4 vols.; Washington: Library of Congress, 1942-43.

j. Conover, Helen Field, *New Zealand: A Selected List of References.* Washington: Library of Congress, 1942. 68 pp.

k. Works dealing with British America published 1902, 1903, 1906-35, 1939-40 included in *Writings on American History.* (See 2-J-1-c, below.)

l. Born, Lester Kruger, *A Checklist of the Microfilms Prepared in England and Wales for the American Council of Learned Societies, 1941-1945.* Washington: Library of Congress, 1955. xvii, 179 pp.

m. *English Books, 1475-1640: A Cross Index by STC Number and Partial List of Microfilms.* Ann Arbor, Mich.: University Microfilms, 1936- . Annual, with cumulation anticipated.

2. Current publications.

a. Milne, Alexander Taylor, *Writings on British History* . . . . London: Jonathan Cape, 1937- . Covering books published each year since 1934.

b. Frewer, Louis Benson, *Bibliography of Historical Writings Published in Great Britain and the Empire, 1940-1945.* Oxford: B. Blackwell, 1947. xx, 346 pp. Index.

c. *The English Historical Review, The Canadian Historical Review, Historical Studies of Australia and New Zealand,* and *The American Historical Review* for reviews of books and lists of articles published later than those included in any of the other bibliographical aids in this field.

3. Special topics.

a. Gross, Charles, *A Bibliography of British Municipal History* . . . . New York & London: Longmans, Green & Co., 1897. xxxiv, 461 pp. Index.

b. Hall, Hubert, *A Select Bibliography for the Study, Sources, and Literature of English Mediaeval Economic History.* London: P. S. King & Son, 1914. xiii, 350 pp.

c. Matthews, William, *British Autobiographies: An Annotated Bibliography of British Autobiographies Published or Written before 1951.* Berkeley: University of California Press, 1955. xiv, 367 pp.; and *Ibid., Canadian Diaries and Autobiographies. Ibid.,* 1950. 130 pp. Subject index.

4. Bibliographical references.

a. Clark, George Norman, ed., *The Oxford History of England.* 14 vols. projected; Oxford: Clarendon Press, 1934- .

b. Hunt, William, and Reginald Lane Poole, eds., *The Political History of England.* 12 vols.; London & New York: Longmans, Green & Co., 1905-10.

c. Lunt, William Edward, *History of England.* 4th ed.; New York: Harper & Bros., 1957. Bibl. pp. 897-964.

d. Smith, Goldwin Albert, *A History of England.* New York: Charles Scribner's Sons, c. 1949. Bibl. pp. 832-62.

5. Aids.

a. Stephen, Leslie, and Sidney Lee, eds., *Dictionary of National Biography.* 22 vols.; New York: Macmillan Co., London: Smith, Elder & Co., 1908-1909. With decennial supplements since 1900. See also *The Dictionary of National Biography: The Concise Dictionary . . . to 1930 . . . .* London: Oxford University Press, c. 1939, vii, 1456, 183 pp.

b. *Who's Who . . . .* London: Allen & Unwin, New York: Macmillan Co., etc., 1849- . Annual volumes. With necrologies, *Who Was Who. . . .* Vol. I, 1897-1915; II 1916-28; III, 1929-40; IV, 1941-50.

c. Haydn, Joseph Timothy, and Horace Ockerby, *The Book of Dignities . . . .* 3d ed.; London: W. H. Allen Co., Ltd., 1894, xxviii, 1170 pp. Index.

d. *The Annual Register,* 1758- . General index, 1758-1819.

e. Harvey, Paul, ed., *The Oxford Companion to English Literature.* 3d ed.; Oxford: Clarendon Press, 1946. viii, 931 pp.

f. Barnhart, Clarence Lewis, and William D. Halsey, eds., *The New Century Handbook of English Literature.* New York: Appleton-Century-Crofts, 1956. vii, 1167 pp.

F. Slavic Europe and Russia

1. Guides and bibliographies.

a. Morley, Charles, *Guide to Research in Russian History.* Syracuse, N. Y.: Syracuse University Press, c. 1951. xiii, 227 pp.

b. Kovalevsky, Pierre, *Manuel d'histoire russe . . . .* Paris: Payot, 1948. 349 pp.

c. Kerner, Robert Joseph, *Slavic Europe: A Selected Bibliography in the Western European Languages . . . .* Cambridge, Mass.: Harvard University Press, 1918. 402 pp.

d. Grierson, Philip, *Books on Soviet Russia, 1917-1942: A Bibliography and a Guide to Reading.* London: Methuen & Co., c. 1943.

e. Dorosh, John Thomas, *Guide to Soviet Bibliographies: A Selected List of References.* Washington: Library of Congress, 1950. v, 158 pp.

f. Conover, Helen Field, *The Balkans . . . A Selected List of References.* 5 vols.; Washington: Library of Congress, 1943.

2. Historiographies.

a. Mazour, Anatole Grigorevich, *An Outline of Modern Russian Historiography.* Berkeley: University of California Press, 1939. ix, 130 pp. Gen. bibl. pp. 123-26, index.

b. Karpovich, Michael, "The Russian Revolution of 1917," *The Journal of Modern History,* II (June 1930) , 258-80.

c. Sherkan, Alfred A., "Modern Russian Historiography," *Kent* (Ohio) *State University Bulletin, Research Series,* I (1952) , 37-60.

3. Current publications.

a. *The Slavonic and East European Review.* London, 1922- . Title varies.
b. *The American Slavic and East European Review.* 1942- .

c. *The Russian Review.* Hanover, N. H., 1942- . July issues have annual bibliographies of books and articles on Russia.

d. *Problems of Communism.* Washington: U. S. Information Agency, 1952- .

e. Smits, Rudolf, *Serial Publications of the Soviet Union, 1939-1957: A Bibliographic Checklist.* Washington: Government Printing Office, 1958. ix, 459 pp.

4. Bibliographical references.

a. Pares, Bernard, *A History of Russia.* Definitive ed.; New York: Alfred A. Knopf, 1953. Bibl. by E. Buist, pp. 583-611.

b. Harcave, Sidney Samuel, *Russia: A History.* 3d ed.; Philadelphia: J. P. Lippincott & Co., c. 1952. Bibl. pp. i-xvi.

c. Mayo, Henry Bertram, *Democracy and Marxism.* New York: Oxford University Press, 1955. Bibl. 339-53.

d. Seton-Watson, Hugh, *From Lenin to Malenkov* . . . . New York: Frederick A. Praeger, Inc., 1953. Bibl. 357-68.

e. Carr, Edward Hallett, *A History of Soviet Russia.* 4 vols.; London: Macmillan Co., Ltd., New York: St. Martin's Press, 1950-1954. Bibl. III, 567-85, IV, 377-79.

f. Harkins, William Edward, *Dictionary of Russian Literature.* New York: Philosophical Library, c. 1956. vi, 439 pp.

g. Rubinchek, Leonid Selik and Leona W. Eisele, *A Digest of the Krasnyi Arkhiv* . . . . 2 vols.; Cleveland: Cleveland Public Library [etc.], 1947-55.

h. *Istoriia SSSR: Ukazatel' sovetskoi literatury* [History of the USSR: Index of Soviet Literature], *1917-1952.* 3 vols. planned. Moscow: Academy of Sciences, 1956- . Volume I, with separate supplement, covers period to 1861.

5. Aids.

a. Strakhovsky, Leonid Ivan, *A Handbook of Slavic Studies.* Cambridge, Mass.: Harvard University Press, 1949. xxi, 753 pp. Bibls.

b. Rouček, Joseph Slabey, ed., *Slavonic Encylopaedia.* New York: Philosophical Library, 1949. xi, 1445 pp.

c. Freund, Henry Alexander, *Russia from A to Z* . . . . Sydney & London: Angus & Robertson, Ltd., 1945. 713 pp. Bibl. pp. 603-65, index.

6. Atlases.

a. *Historical Atlas of the USSR.* 3 vols.; New York: C. S. Hammond & Co., 1950.

b. Goodall, George, *Soviet Union in Maps* . . . . London: George Philip & Son, Ltd., Chicago: Denoyer-Geppert Co., 1954. In colors. 32 pp. $1.25.

c. *Oxford Regional Economic Atlas: U. S. S. R.* New York: Oxford University Press, 1957. 142 pp. Paper bound $5.75.

G. Near East and Africa

1. Guides and bibliographies.

a. Ettinghausen, Richard, ed., *A Selected and Annotated Bibliography of Books and Periodicals in Western Languages Dealing with the Near and Middle East with Special Emphasis on Medieval and Modern Times.* (With supplement.) Washington: Middle East Institute, 1954. viii, 137 pp.

b. Birge, John Kingsley, *A Guide to Turkish Area Study.* Washington: American Council of Learned Societies, 1949. xii, 240 pp. Maps, geneal. table.

c. Elwell-Sutton, Laurence Paul, *A Guide to Iranian Area Study.* Ann Arbor, Mich.: J. W. Edwards for the American Council of Learned Societies, 1952. 235 pp.

d. Gabrieli, Giuseppe, *Manuale di bibliografia musulmana* . . . . Pt. 1; Rome: Tipografia dell' Unione editrice, 1916. 489 pp.

e. Koray, Enver, *Türkiye Tarih Yayinlari Bibliyografyasi* [Bibliography of Publications on History in Turkey], *1729-1950.* Ankara: Millî Eğitim Basimevi, 1952. 548 pp.

f. Masson, Paul, *Eléments d'une bibliographie française de la Syrie* . . . . Paris: E. Champion, 1919. 528 pp.

g. Melzig, Herbert, *Bibliographie universelle de la Turquie nouvelle.* Istanbul: Ulkü Kitap Yurdu, 1944. 223 pp.

h. Human Relations Area Files, Inc. (HRAF), *Handbooks and Annotated Bibliographies.* New Haven, Conn.: Human Relations Area Files, 1956- . On various Arab countries and Iran and Afghanistan.

i. *Palestine and Zionism: A Cumulative Author, Title, and Subject Index to Books, Pamphlets, and Periodicals.* 2 vols.; New York: Palestine Foundation Fund, 1946.

j. Pfannmüller, Gustav, *Handbuch der Islam-Literatur.* Berlin & Leipzig: W. de Gruyter & Co., 1923. viii, 436 pp.

k. Thomsen, Peter, *Die Palästina-Literatur* . . . . 5 vols.; Leipzig: J. C. Hinrichs, 1911-37.

l. Farman, Hafez Fitzhugh, *Iran: A Selected and Annotated Bibliography.* Washington: Library of Congress, 1951. ix, 100 pp.

m. U. S., Library of Congress, Orientalia Division, *The Arabian Peninsula: A Selected Annotated List of Periodicals, Books, and Articles in English.* Washington: Library of Congress, 1951. xi, 111 pp.

n. U. S., Department of State, *Point Four: Near East and Africa. A Selected Bibliography* . . . . Washington: Government Printing Office, 1951. ii, 136 pp.

o. Weber, Shirley Howard, *Voyages and Travels in Greece, the Near East, and Adjacent Regions Made Previous to the Year 1801* . . . . Princeton, N. J.: American School of Classical Studies, 1953. vii, 208 pp.

p. Weber, Shirley Howard, *Voyages and Travels in the Near East Made during the XIX Century* . . . . Princeton, N. J.: American School of Classical Studies, 1952. x, 252 pp.

q. Wilson, Arnold Talbot, *A Bibliography of Persia.* Oxford: Clarendon Press, 1930. x, 253 pp.

r. Sauvaget, Jean, *Introduction à l'histoire de l'Orient musulman* . . . . Paris: Adrien-Maisonneuve, 1943. 202 pp.

s. Conover, Helen Field, *Introduction to Africa: A Selective Guide to Background Reading.* Washington: Library of Congress, 1952. lx, 237 pp.

t. Conover, Helen Field, *Africa South of the Sahara: A Selected and Annotated List of Writings, 1951-1956.* Washington: Library of Congress, 1957. vii, 269 pp.

u. Conover, Helen Field, *Research and Information on Africa: Continuing Sources.* Washington: Library of Congress, 1954, reprinted 1957. vi, 70 pp.

2. Bibliographical references.

a. Brockelmann, Carl, *History of the Islamic Peoples.* New York: G. P. Putnam's Sons, c. 1947. xx, 582 pp. Maps, bibl. pp. 539-49, index.

b. Lewis, Bernard, *The Arabs in History.* London & New York: Hutchinson's University Library, 1950. 196 pp. Maps, bibl. pp. 184-88, index.

c. Gibb, Hamilton Alexander Rosskeen, *Mohammedanism: An Historical Survey.* 2d ed.; London & New York: Oxford University Press, 1953. ix, 206 pp. Bibl. pp. 192-200, index. Also reprinted in Mentor Books.

d. Kirk, George Edward, *A Short History of the Middle East from the Rise of*

Islam to Modern Times. 4th ed. rev.; London: Methuen Co., New York: Frederick A. Praeger, c. 1957. 308 pp. Maps, bibl., index.

   e. Schevill, Ferdinand and Wesley M. Gewehr, *The History of the Balkan Peninsula.* Rev. ed.; New York: Harcourt, Brace & Co., c. 1933. vii, 614 pp. Bibls., index.

   f. Wolff, Robert Lee, *The Balkans in Our Time.* Cambridge, Mass.: Harvard University Press, 1956. xxi, 618 pp. Maps, tables.

   g. Lenczowski, George, *The Middle East in World Affairs.* 2d. ed.; Ithaca, N. Y.: Cornell University Press, c. 1956. Maps, bibl. pp. 548-65.

3. Current publications.

   a. *The Middle East Journal* and *The American Historical Review* for reviews of books and lists of articles.

4. Aids and atlases.

   a. *The Encyclopaedia of Islam . . . .* 4 vols. and supplement; Leyden: Brill, London: Luzac & Co., 1913-38. Rev. ed. now appearing in fascicules.

   b. Pareja Casañas, Félix M., *Islamologia.* 2 vols.; Madrid: Editiorial Razón y Fe, 1952-54.

   c. Fisher, William Bayne, *The Middle East: A Physical, Social, and Regional Geography.* Rev. ed.; London: Methuen Co., New York: E. P. Dutton & Co., c. 1952. xiii, 514 pp. Maps, charts, diagrs., bibl. pp. 501-505, index.

   d. Hazard, Harry W., *Atlas of Islamic History.* Princeton, N. J.: Princeton University Press, 1954. 49 pp.

   e. Roolvink, Roelof, *et al., Historical Atlas of the Muslim Peoples.* Cambridge, Mass.: Harvard University Press, 1957. x, 40 pages of maps in color.

   f. *Oxford Regional Economic Atlas: The Middle East and North Africa.* New York: Oxford University Press, 1957. 60 pages of maps in color.

H. Far East

1. General.

   a. Quan, Lau-king, *Introduction to Asia: A Selective Guide to Background Reading.* Washington: Library of Congress, 1955. x, 214 pp.

   b. Baqai, I. H., *Books on Asia.* New Delhi: Indian Council of World Affairs, c. 1947. 111 pp.

   c. Philips, Cyril Henry, ed., *Handbook of Oriental History.* London: Royal Historical Society, 1951. viii, 265 pp. Bibls.

   d. Sinor, Denis, ed., *Orientalism and History.* Cambridge: W. Heffer, 1954. viii, 107 pp. Bibl. refs.

   e. Bingham, Woodbridge, and Hilary Conroy, *The History and Civilization of Asia.* 2 vols.; Berkeley: University of California, 1952. Syllabus and bibl. Mimeographed.

   f. Clyde, Paul Hibbert, *The Far East . . . .* 2d ed.; New York: Prentice-Hall, Inc., 1958. xxviii, 836 pp. Index. Bibl. at end of each chapter.

   g. Sellman, Roger Raymond, *An Outline Atlas of Eastern History.* London: Edward Arnold, Ltd., c. 1954. 63 pp.

   h. Müller, Frederick Max, ed., *The Sacred Books of the East.* 50 vols.; Oxford: Clarendon Press, 1879-1910.

2. Current publications.

   a. *Bulletin of Far Eastern Bibliography,* 1936-40. Washington: American Council of Learned Societies. Continued as part of

b. *The Far Eastern Quarterly,* 1941-46; and since 1946 issued as annual supplement. Enlarged in 1956 to become

c. *The Journal of Asian Studies.* With annual bibliographical supplement.

3. India and Southeast Asia.

a. Moraes, George Mark, *Bibliography of Indological Studies.* Bombay: Examiner Press, 1945. 188 pp.

b. Dowson, John, *A Classical Dictionary of Hindu Mythology and Religion, Geography, History, and Literature.* 6th ed.; London: K. Paul, Trench, Trubner & Co., 1928. xix, 411 pp.

c. Embree, John Fee, and Lillian Ota Dotson, *Bibliography of the Peoples and Cultures of Mainland Southeast Asia.* New Haven, Conn.: Yale University Press, 1950. xxxiii, 821 pp. Maps.

d. Hobbs, Cecil Carleton, *Southeast Asia: An Annotated Bibliography* . . . . Washington: Library of Congress, 1952. 163 pp.

e. Hall, Daniel George Edward, *A History of South-East Asia.* New York: St. Martin's Press, c. 1955. Bibl. pp. 763-89.

f. Brown, William Norman, *The United States and India and Pakistan.* Cambridge, Mass.: Harvard University Press, 1953. Intro. bibl. pp. 291-97.

g. Rapson, Edward James, *et al., Cambridge History of India.* 6 vols. planned — II (100-1100 A.D.) never published; Cambridge: Cambridge University Press, 1922-37. Bibls. at ends of vols.

h. Majumdar, Ramesh Chandra, ed., *The History and Culture of the Indian People.* 10 vols. planned; London: Allen & Unwin, 1951- . Bibls. at ends of vols.

i. Majumdar, Ramesh Chandra, *et al., An Advanced History of India.* 2d ed.; London: Macmillan Ltd., 1950. Bibl. pp. 265-72, 617-26, 1023-41.

j. Davies, Cuthbert Collin, *An Historical Atlas of the Indian Peninsula.* New York: Oxford University Press, c. 1953. 94 pp.

4. Northeast Asia.

a. Kerner, Robert Joseph, *Northeastern Asia: A Selected Bibliography* . . . . 2 vols.; Berkeley: University of California Press, 1939.

5. China.

a. Goodrich, Luther Carrington, and H. C. Fenn, *A Syllabus of the History of Chinese Civilization and Culture.* New York: China Society of America, c. 1947. 55 pp.

b. Gardner, Charles Sidney, *A Union List of Selected Western Books on China in American Libraries.* 2d ed., rev. and enl.; Washington: American Council of Learned Societies, c. 1938. xi, 111 pp. Author index.

c. Cordier, Henri, *Bibliotheca sinica.* 5 vols.; Paris: E. Guilmoto, 1904-24.

d. Latourette, Kenneth Scott, *The Chinese: Their History and Culture.* 3d ed.; New York: Macmillan Co., 1946. xvi, 847 pp. Bibls. at ends of chapters.

e. Rostow, Walt Whitman, *et al., The Prospects for Communist China.* Cambridge, Mass.: Technology Press of Massachusetts Institute of Technology, c. 1954. Bibl. pp. 327-74.

f. Fairbank, John King, *The United States and China.* Rev. ed.; Cambridge, Mass.: Harvard University Press, 1958. Interpretative bibl. pp. 321-44.

g. Herrmann, Albert, *Historical and Commercial Atlas of China.* Cambridge, Mass.: Harvard University Press, 1935. 112 pp.

h. *China Year Book,* New York: E. P. Dutton & Co., 1912-19; Tientsin: Tientsin Press, 1921-29; Shanghai: North China Daily News, 1931-39.

i. Couling, Samuel, *The Encyclopaedia Sinica.* Shanghai, etc.: Kelly & Walsh, Ltd., 1917. viii, 633 pp.

j. Gardner, Charles Sidney, *Chinese Traditional Historiography.* Cambridge, Mass.: Harvard University Press, 1938. xi, 120 pp. Bibl. footnotes.

k. Yang, Lien-sheng, *Topics in Chinese History.* Cambridge, Mass.: Harvard University Press, 1950. vii, 57 pp. Bibls.

l. Hightower, James Robert, *Topics in Chinese Literature: Outlines and Bibliographies.* Rev. ed.; Cambridge, Mass.: Harvard University Press, 1953. ix, 141 pp.

m. Frankel, Hans H., *Catalogue of Translations from the Chinese Dynastic Histories for the Period 220-960.* Berkeley: University of California Press, 1957. 295 pp. Indexes.

n. Fairbank, John King, and Kwang-ching Liu, *Modern China: A Bibliographical Guide to Chinese Works, 1898-1937.* Cambridge Mass.: Harvard University Press, 1950. xviii, 608 pp.

o. Têng, Ssŭ-Yü, and Knight Biggerstaff, *An Annotated Bibliography of Selected Chinese Works.* Rev. ed.; Cambridge, Mass.: Harvard University Press, 1950, x, 326 pp.

6. Japan.

a. Borton, Hugh, *et al., A Selected List of Books and Articles on Japan in English, French, and German.* Washington: American Council of Learned Societies, c. 1940. x, 142 pp.

b. Borton, Hugh, *Japan's Modern Century.* New York: Ronald Press Co., c. 1955. Bibl. pp. 468-82.

c. Uyehara, Cecil H., and Edwin G. Beal, *Checklist of Archives in the Japanese Ministry of Foreign Affairs, Tokyo, Japan, 1868-1945, Microfilmed for the Library of Congress, 1949-1951.* Washington: Library of Congress, 1954. xii, 262 pp.

7. Pacific.

a. Conover, Helen Field, *Islands of the Pacific: A Selected List of References.* Washington: Library of Congress, 1943. 154 pp.

b. Hardy, Osgood, and Glenn S. Dumke, *A History of the Pacific Area in Modern Times.* Boston, etc.: Houghton Mifflin Co., c. 1949. Bibl. pp. 711-24.

c. Taylor, Clyde Romer Hughes, *A Pacific Bibliography: Printed Matter Relating to the Native Peoples of Polynesia, Melanesia, and Micronesia.* Wellington, N. Z.: Polynesian Society, 1951. xxix, 492 pp. Index, map.

d. Lietz, Paul S., *Calendar of Philippine Documents in the Ayer Collection of the Newberry Library.* Chicago: Newberry Library, 1956. xvi, 259 pp.

I. United States

1. Bibliographies.

a. Handlin, Oscar, *et al., Harvard Guide to American History.* Cambridge, Mass.: Belknap Press of Harvard University Press, 1954. xxiv, 689 pp. $10.00. Detailed bibliographies, mostly unannotated; bibliographies in special fields, pp. 106-108; for government documents, pp. 112-49. Unusually full index, pp. 547-689. Successor to the still somewhat useful Channing, Edward, Albert Bushnell Hart, and Frederick Jackson Turner, *Guide to the Study and Reading of American History.* Rev. and augm. ed.; Boston & London: Ginn & Co., 1912. xvi, 650 pp.

b. Beers, Henry Putney, *Bibliographies in American History: Guide to Materials for Research.* New York: H. W. Wilson Co., 1942. xv, 487 pp.

c. *Writings on American History,* 1902, 1903, 1906-40, 1948- .

(1) Richardson, Ernest Cushing, and Anson Ely Morse, *Writings on American History, 1902.* Princeton, N. J.: Library Book Store, 1904. xxi, 294 pp.

(2) McLaughlin, Andrew Cunningham, *et al., Writings on American History, 1903.* Washington: Carnegie Institution, 1905. xiv, 172 pp.

(3) Griffin, Grace Gardner, *Writings . . . ,* 1906 through 1940. Annual volumes, 1906-36, biennial 1937-40. Volumes for 1906-1908 published New York: Macmillan Co., 1908-10; 1909-11, Washington: Government Printing Office, 1911-13; 1912-17, New Haven, Conn.: Yale University Press, 1914-19; 1918-40 published as supplementary volumes of the American Historical Association, *Annual Report* for appropriate years. Volumes through 1935 also cover British America and Latin America; volume for 1939-40 covers British America. Cumulative *Index to the Writings on American History, 1902-1940.* Washington: American Historical Association, 1956. vii, 1115 pp. Made possible by the bequest of David Maydole Matteson and prepared for publication by William Columbus Davis. Plans are under way for a selective list to fill the gap for 1941-47.

(4) Masterson, James E., *Writings . . . ,* 1948- , continued as supplementary volumes of the A. H. A., *Annual Report.* For the gap referred to above and since the most recent Masterson volume consult book reviews and lists of articles in *The American Historical Review.*

d. Bemis, Samuel Flagg, and Grace Gardner Griffin, *Guide to the Diplomatic History of the United States, 1775-1921.* Washington: Government Printing Office, 1935. xvii, 979 pp. Index.

e. Larson, Henrietta Melia, *Guide to Business History . . . .* Cambridge, Mass.: Harvard University Press, 1948. xxvi, 1181 pp.

f. Matthews, William, *American Diaries . . . Written Prior to the Year 1861.* Berkeley & Los Angeles: University of California Press, 1945. xiv. 383 pp.

g. Swem, Earl Gregg, *Virginia Historical Index.* 2 vols.; Roanoke, Va.: Stone Printing & Mfg. Co., 1934-36.

h. Easterby, James Harold, *Guide to the Study and Reading of South Carolina History: A General Classified Bibliography.* 2 pts.; Columbia: Historical Commission of South Carolina, 1949-50 [i.e., 1953].

i. Larned, Josephus Nelson, ed., *The Literature of American History: A Bibliographic Guide . . . .* Boston: Houghton Mifflin Co., 1902. ix, 596 pp. Continued by Philip P. Wells in *Titles of Books on English and American History.* New York: American Library Assoc., 1904, and in A. L. A. *Booklist,* Feb. 1906.

j. *A Report on World Population Migrations as Related to the United States of America.* Washington: George Washington University, c. 1956. Historical bibliography, pp. 85-295, by Richard Catlin Haskett.

2. Periodical indexes.

a. Griffin, Appleton Prentiss Clark, *Bibliography of American Historical Societies,* published as Vol. II of the American Historical Association, *Annual Report, 1905.* Washington: Government Printing Office, 1907. 1374 pp. Index and index of societies.

b. *Poole's Index to Periodical Literature.* (See 2-A-3-b, p. 14, above.)

c. *Reader's Guide to Periodical Literature.* (See 2-A-3-c, above.)

d. *American Periodical Series.* Ann Arbor, Mich.: University Microfilms, 1947- . Annual. Cumulation anticipated.

e. Haskell, Daniel C., *The Nation, Volumes 1-105, New York, 1865-1917: Index of Titles and Contributors.* 2 vols.; New York: New York Public Library, 1951-53.

f. Mott, Frank Luther, *A History of American Magazines.* 4 vols. to date; Cambridge, Mass.: Harvard University Press, 1939- .

g. Doll, Eugene Edgar, *The Pennsylvania Magazine of History and Biography: Index, Volumes 1-75 (1877-1951)*. Philadelphia: Historical Society of Pennsylvania, 1954. xv, 1170 pp. Oldest existing historical magazine in the United States.

h. Leary, Lewis Gaston, *Articles on American Literature, 1900-1950*. Durham, N. C.: Duke University Press, 1954. 437 pp.

3. Newspaper indexes.

a. Cappon, Lester Jesse, and Stella F. Duff, *Virginia Gazette Index, 1736-1780.* 2 vols.; Williamsburg, Va.: Institute of Early American History and Culture, 1950. The newspaper itself can be obtained on microfilm at a modest cost.

b. *The New York Times Index.* (See 2-A-4-c, pp. 14-15, above.)

c. *New York Daily Tribune Index.* (See 2-A-4-d, above.)

d. Brayer, Herbert O., "Preliminary Guide to Indexed Newspapers in the United States, 1850-1900," *MVHR*, XXXIII (Sept. 1946), 237-58. (See 2-A-4-g, above.)

e. Cohen, Hennig, *The South Carolina Gazette, 1732-1775*. Columbia: University of South Carolina Press, 1953. xv, 273 pp. A microfilm copy of all extant South Carolina newspapers, 1732-82, is obtainable from the Charleston Library Society in 12 reels for $150.00.

f. Footnotes in Carl Bridenbaugh, *Cities in the Wilderness* (reissue) and *Cities in Revolt* (notes issued separately in mimeographed form). New York: Alfred A. Knopf, 1955. Refer, by subject, to all colonial newspapers.

4. Government documents.

a. Boyd, Anne Morris, *United States Government Publications* . . . . 3d ed., rev. by Rae Elizabeth Rips. New York: H. W. Wilson Co., 1949 [i.e., 1952]. xx, 627 pp. Bibls.

b. Schmeckebier, Laurence Frederick, ed., *Government Publications and Their Use.* 2d rev. ed.; Washington: Brookings Institution, 1939. xv, 479 pp.

c. Poore, Benjamin Perley, *A Descriptive Catalogue of the Government Publications of the United States, September 5, 1774-March 4, 1881* (Senate Misc. Doc. 67, 48th Cong., 2d Sess.). Washington: Government Printing Office, 1885, and Ann Arbor, Mich.: J. W. Edwards, 1953. iv, 1392 pp. Continued by John Griffith Ames, *Comprehensive Index to the Publications of the United States, 1881-1893* (House Document 754, 58th Cong., 2d Sess.). 2 vols.; Washington: Government Printing Office, 1905; 2 vols. in 1; Ann Arbor, Mich.: J. W. Edwards, 1953. v, 1590 pp. Further continued by each Congress in *Catalog of the Public Documents* . . . . 25 vols.; Washington: Government Printing Office, 1896-1945. From 1940 it is necessary to use the *Monthly Catalog of United States Government Publications*. Title varies. Washington: Government Printing Office, 1895- .

5. Manuscripts.

a. *Guide to the Records in the National Archives.* Washington: Government Printing Office, 1948. xiv, 684 pp. Appdcs., index. With supplements. See also *List of National Archives Microfilm Publications, 1953,* with supplements. Particularly useful is *Federal Population Censuses, 1840-1880: A Price List of Microfilm Copies of the Original Population Schedules*. Washington: National Archives and Records Service 1955. vi, 73 pp. See also *A Brief Guide to U. S. Naval Sources in the Washington, D. C. Area*. Washington 25: Navy Department . . . Naval History Division, 1957. 7 pp.

b. Garrison, Curtis Wiswell, "List of Manuscript Collections in the Library of Congress, July 1931," American Historical Association, *Annual Report for the Year 1930,* I, 123-249; Powell, C. Percy, "List of Manuscript Collections Received in the Library of Congress, July 1931 to July 1938," *Ibid.,* 1937, I, 113-45; *Annual Report of* *the Librarian of Congress*, 1938-42; Library of Congress, *Quarterly Journal of Acquisitions*, 1943- .

c. Griffin, Grace Gardner, *A Guide to Manuscripts Relating to American History in British Repositories Reproduced for the Division of Manuscripts of the Library of Congress*. Washington: Library of Congress, 1946. xvi, 313 pp. Index.

d. Billington, Ray Allen, "Guides to American History Manuscript Collections in Libraries of the United States," *The Mississippi Valley Historical Review*, XXXVIII (Dec. 1951), 467-96.

e. Between 1907 and 1937 the Carnegie Institution of Washington brought out a number of guides to materials for American history in archives in Great Britain, Canada, Spain, Mexico, Cuba, France, Germany, Austria, Switzerland, Italy, and Russia. See Handlin, *et al., Harvard Guide* (2-I-1-a, above), pp. 87-88.

f. Most of the state archives and the principal repositories of privately originated manuscript collections have prepared printed or mimeographed listings of their holdings. Information may be obtained by direct correspondence if you cannot find it otherwise. The National Historical Publications Commission, with Philip May Hamer of the National Archives as Executive Director, will shortly publish *A Guide to Depositories of Archives and Manuscripts in the United States* which will describe the more important holdings of some 1,300 institutions. The issues of *The American Historical Review* and regional and state historical journals carry notices of the more important recent acquisitions. The Historical Records Survey of the Works Progress Administration inventoried many county and municipal archives. See Child, Sargent Bunage, and Dorothy P. Holmes, *Bibliography of Research Projects Reports: Check List of Historical Records Survey Publications*, Works Progress Administration, *Technical Series Research and Records Bibliography, No. 7*. Washington: Government Printing Office, 1943. 110 pp.; and Colby, Merle E., "Final Report on Disposition of Unpublished Materials of the W. P. A. Writers Program." In typescript, 1943. 12 pp. Copies of virtually all of these publications are now out of print but are, along with the Child and Holmes and the Colby check lists, available in the Interior Section of the National Archives, with which arrangements may be made to obtain microfilm or photostatic reproductions. See also Handlin, *et al., Harvard Guide* (2-I-1-a, above), pp. 79-88.

g. Jenkins, William Sumner, and Lillian A. Hamrick, *A Guide to Microfilm Collections of Early State Records*. Washington: Library of Congress, 1950. xxxviii, 308, 206, 44, 101, 56, 9, 38 pp. And *Supplement*, 1951. xxiii, 130, xxviii.

h. Greene, Evarts Boutell, and Richard Brandon Morris, *A Guide to the Principal Sources for Early American History (1600-1800) in the City of New York*. 2d ed.; New York: Columbia University Press, 1953. xxxvi, 400 pp.

6. Reference works and aids.

a. Johnson, Allen, and Dumas Malone, eds., *Dictionary of American Biography*. New York: Charles Scribner's Sons, 1928-37. 21 vols., including index vol.; Starr, Harris E., ed., *Dictionary of American Biography, Supplement One*, to 31 December 1935. Charles Scribner's Sons, 1944. 718 pp.; Schuyler, Robert Livingston, and Edward Topping James, . . . *Supplement Two*, to 31 December 1940. *Ibid.*, 1958. A condensed volume covering the whole is under way.

b. *Who's Who in America*. Chicago: Marquis-Who's-Who, 1897- . Biennial. *Who Was Who in America*. Vol. I, 1897-1942, Vol. II, 1943-1950; Chicago: A. N. Marquis Co., 1943, 1950.

c. Cattell, Jaques, ed., *Directory of American Scholars: A Biographical Directory*. 3d ed.; New York: R. R. Bowker Co., 1957. x, 836 pp.; *American Men of Science: A Biographical Directory*. 9th ed.; 3 vols.; Lancaster, Pa.: Science Press, New York: R. R. Bowker Co., 1955-56. Vol. I. *The Physical Sciences*, Vol. II. *The Biological Sciences*, Vol. III. *The Social and Behavioral Sciences*.

d. *Biographical Directory of the American Congress, 1774-1949.* Washington: Government Printing Office, 1950. 2057 pp. See also *Directory* for each Congress and annual *U. S. Army Register, U. S. Navy Register,* and *U. S. Air Force Register.*

e. Morris, Richard Brandon, ed., *Encyclopedia of American History.* New York: Harper & Bros., c. 1953. xv, 776 pp. Maps, diagrs. Adams, James Truslow, and R. V. Coleman, eds., *Dictionary of American History.* 5 vols., incl. index vol.; New York: Charles Scribner's Sons, 1940.

f. *Historical Statistics of the United States, 1789-1945: A Supplement to the Statistical Abstract of the United States.* Washington: Government Printing Office, 1949. viii, 363 pp. Index. *The Statistical Abstract* is published annually by the GPO.

g. *The World Almanac and Book of Facts,* 1869-77, 1887- . Also *Information Please Almanac,* 1947- . Both annual.

h. Spiller, Robert Ernest, *et al., Literary History of the United States: Bibliography.* New York: Macmillan Co., 1948. xxii, 817 pp. Index.

i. Blanck, Jacob Nathaniel, *Bibliography of American Literature.* New Haven, Conn.: Yale University Press, 1955- . Vol. II, to "Timothy Dwight."

j. Hart, James David, *The Oxford Companion to American Literature.* 3rd ed. rev. and enl.; New York: Oxford University Press, 1956. viii, 890 pp. Chronological index.

k. Hubbell, Jay Broadus, *The South in American Literature, 1607-1900.* Durham, N. C.: Duke University Press, 1954. Bibl. pp. 883-974.

l. Mathews, Mitford McLeod, ed., *A Dictionary of Americanisms on Historical Principles.* Chicago: University of Chicago Press, c. 1951. xvi, 1946 pp.

m. [Plotkin, David George] David Kin, *A Dictionary of American Maxims.* New York: Philosophical Library, c. 1955. 597 pp.

n. Groce, George Cuthbert and David H. Wallace, *Dictionary of Artists in America, 1564-1860.* New Haven, Conn.: Yale University Press, 1957. xxvii, 759 pp.

7. Atlases.

a. Paullin, Charles Oscar, *Atlas of the Historical Geography of the United States.* Washington: Carnegie Institution, New York: American Geographical Society, 1932. xv, 162 pp., 166 plates. Index.

b. Adams, James Truslow, and R. V. Coleman, eds., *Atlas of American History.* New York: Charles Scribner's Sons, c. 1943. xi, 360 pp., 147 plates. Index.

c. Lord, Clifford Lee, and Elizabeth H. Lord, *Historical Atlas of the United States.* New York: Henry Holt & Co., c. 1944. xix, 264 pp., 217 maps. Appdcs., index. Paper bound $3.25.

d. Wesley, Edgar B., *Our United States: Its History in Maps.* Chicago: Denoyer-Geppert Co., c. 1956. 96 pp. Paper bound $2.00.

e. *Hammond's American History Atlas.* Maplewood, N. J.: C. S. Hammond & Co., 1957. 40 pp. Paper bound $0.50.

J. Latin America

1. Bibliographies.

a. *Handbook of Latin American Studies* . . . . Cambridge: Harvard University Press, 1936-47; Gainesville: University of Florida Press, 1948- . Annual, beginning with 1935.

b. *Writings on American History.* (See 2-I-1-c, p. 27, above.) Volumes 1902, 1903, 1906-35 cover Latin America.

c. *A Guide to the Official Publications of the Other American Republics.* 18 vols.; Washington: Library of Congress, Hispanic Foundation, 1945-48. There is one volume for each Latin American republic except Mexico and Nicaragua.

d. Jones, Cecil Knight, *A Bibliography of Latin American Bibliographies.* 2d ed.; Washington: Government Printing Office, 1942. 311 pp. Index.

e. Humphreys, Robert [i.e. Robin] Arthur, *Latin America: A Selective Guide to Publications in English.* London & New York: Royal Institute of International Affairs, c. 1949. viii, 63 pp. Appdx. New ed., *Latin American History: A Guide to the Literature in English.* In press.

f. Wilgus, Alva Curtis, *Histories and Historians of Hispanic America.* New York: H. W. Wilson Co., 1942. xii, 144 pp.

2. Current publications.

a. *The Hispanic American Historical Review* and *The American Historical Review* contain reviews of books and lists of articles since the latest issue of 2-J-1-a, above. See also Ruth Lapham Butler, *Guide to the Hispanic American Historical Review, 1918-1945.* Durham, N. C.: Duke University Press, 1950. xviii, 251 pp.

b. *Revista de historia de América.* Mexico, D. F.: Instituto Panamericano de Geografía e Historia, 1938- . Quarterly.

c. *Revista interamericana de bibliografía.* Washington: Pan American Union, 1949- . Quarterly.

d. *Américas.* Washington: Pan American Union, 1949- . Monthly. English, Spanish and Portuguese editions.

e. *Índice histórico español.* Barcelona: Editorial Teide, for the University of Barcelona, 1953- . Republished biennually in bound volumes as *Bibliografía histórica de España e Hispanoamérica.*

3. Periodical indexes.

a. *Poole's Index to Periodical Literature.* (See 2-A-3-b, p. 14, above.)
b. *Reader's Guide to Periodical Literature.* (See 2-A-3-c, above.)
c. *International Index to Periodicals.* (See 2-A-3-d, above.)

4. Newspaper indexes.

a. *The Official Index to The Times* and *Palmer's Index to "The Times" Newspaper.* (See 2-A-4-b and 2-A-4-a, p. 14, above.)
b. *The New York Times Index.* (See 2-A-4-c, pp. 14-15, above.)
c. *New York Daily Tribune Index.* (See 2-A-4-d, above.)

The above indexes are valuable because of the extensive Latin American coverage of these newspapers and also as guides to topics probably treated in leading Latin American dailies.

5. Manuscripts.

a. Hill, Roscoe R., *The National Archives of Latin America.* Cambridge: Harvard University Press, 1945. xx, 169 pp.

b. Hilton, Ronald, *Handbook of Hispanic Source Materials and Research Organizations in the United States.* 2d ed.; Stanford, Calif.: Stanford University Press, 1956. xiv, 448 pp. Index.

c. *Guide to the Records in the National Archives.* Washington: Government Printing Office, 1948. xvi, 648 pp. Appdcs., index. With supplements.

d. Manuscript Division, Library of Congress. (See 2-I-5-b, pp. 28-29, above.)

6. Aids.

a. Martin, Percy Alvin, *Who's Who in Latin America.* 3rd ed., rev. and enl.; 7 vols.; Chicago: A. N. Marquis Co., London: Oxford University Press, 1946-51. By areas.

b. *Bibliography of Selected Statistical Sources of the American Nations.* Washington: Inter-American Statistical Institute, 1947. xvi, 689 pp.

3 | NOTE TAKING

> *"Why," said the Gryphon, "you first form into a line along the sea-shore —"*
> *"Two lines!" cried the Mock Turtle. "Seals, turtles, salmon, and so on: then, when you've cleared all the jelly-fish out of the way —"*
> Lewis Carroll, *Alice's Adventures in Wonderland*, "The Lobster-Quadrille."

A proper note system, for both bibliographical and content notes, is an all but indispensable prerequisite to sound scholarship. Whenever your search brings you upon any item that seems to bear on your subject, first get a general conception of its theme and scope. With a book this normally means reading any prefatory material, examining the table of contents, then turning to the back to run through its bibliography, if it has one, and, finally, scanning the text, paying particular attention to the opening and concluding paragraphs of each chapter and to the topic sentences of other paragraphs. You will deal with an article or other short item in much the same way as you would a chapter, but somewhat more intensively.

1. Bibliographical cards. As soon as you are assured that an item will contribute materially to your investigation, make a bibliographical card for it. (Experienced historians sometimes also keep a special, or "Nix," file of works found valueless — the "jelly-fish" — as a reminder that they have consulted them.) You will later copy it into your final bibliography and must, therefore, follow the appropriate form in making it out. (See pages 41-47 in Section 5-C, below.) Most historians use 3 x 5 cards for this purpose, lined or unlined according to whether they fill them out with pen or typewriter. Others, however, prefer 4 x 6 or even 5 x 8 cards in order to have more room for comments, and some use cards of different colors to indicate particular categories of material. Cards of any of these standard sizes, with light-weight metal filing boxes and alphabetical divider cards to match, can be procured easily and cheaply. Decide upon *one* size and use only that. Do not use a pencil unless the rules of the library where you are working require it; and in such a case it is generally best to spray with an artists' fixative or to recopy in more permanent form before it becomes illegibly smudged. *This applies also to content notes. See below.*

In addition to the information which you will include in your bibliography, note on each card the particular library in which you used it and the call number for convenience in later rechecking. After you have taken content notes (3-2, below) on the item, use the remainder or back of the card to summarize the author's qualifications and point of view and your evaluation of the contribution that the item will probably make to your investigation. You will later use this information in preparing your annotated bibliography. Do *not*, however, try to make this serve the purpose of the content note or a substitute for it. You may get some assistance in evaluation from reviews of books in *The American Historical Review* and similar journals.

2. Content notes. You will set down in your content notes the substance of the working material that you are able to extract from your sources. First read through an entire chapter or article in order to gain a conception of its perspective and contours. If you find that you need only to note its purport in a general way, make a summary in outline form. If you need to record more detailed memoranda, do so in a series of notes, each of them dealing with a fairly specific point. Should you yield to the temptation to crowd several matters into a single note, you will later find that it contains information needed at different points in your narrative, with unimaginable inconvenience.

Different historians use a great variety of cards and slips of paper, varying to some extent in accordance with their fields of specialization. Choose whatever type is best suited to your own needs and then use it consistently. Do not try to take notes either in a bound notebook or on odd bits of paper. Cards of any of the three standard sizes indicated above for bibliographical notes are resistant to wear, but they are relatively expensive and because of their thickness take up more filing space. Pads of 5 x 8 inch paper are cheap and convenient. Try to use only one slip per note, using one side only, and tearing it off the pad for filing. If you must run over onto a second sheet, staple them together. Avoid paper clips, which are bulky, impede filing, and get lost. For long quotations it may be more convenient to use 8 x 10½ sheets of paper, one side only, which can then be folded to file with your regular sheets.

For convenience in filing: (1) set down in the upper left hand corner of the note the date, either specific or general as appropriate, of the occurrence referred to, followed by (2) the place, specific or general, where it took place, and (3) a caption summarizing the contents of the note that follows. On the next line cite the source, including pages. For example:

Fri., 12 Oct. 1492.   San Salvador (Watling Is., Bahamas?)

Columbus First Sights Land.

    John Knight, *The History of Exploration in America* (New York: Brown Co., 1927), p. 7.

(Summary)

Where you take only a few notes from any book or article, it will probably be more convenient to cite it in your note in precisely the same fashion in which you would refer to it in a footnote in your finished paper. (See 5-D, pages 47-53, below.) If, however, you find it necessary to take numerous notes from the same source, you will probably find that it saves time to note down the source citation in an abbreviated form as you would do in the case of a second or subsequent footnote reference in your final paper. (See 5-D-12, page 52, below.) For example:

Knight, History of Exploration, p. 7.

In the margin indicate, possibly by an abbreviation or symbol, whether you have quoted your source verbatim or have summarized it. Do not use quotation marks, which might lead to confusion as to whether or not they appeared in the original. Verbatim notes should be taken sparingly — only when they may bear on a crucial point or contain a flavor worth preserving. A deletion must never change the meaning. Indicate it, *if within a sentence,* by three dots alternately spaced (thus . . .), and four if it follows a completed sentence (thus. . . .) — the first dot, of course, being the period from the preceding sentence; and four also if your quotation ends in an unfinished sentence (thus . . . .). This is unnecessary at the beginning or end of quotations opening or closing with a full sentence in the original. Check the note immediately to insure accuracy.

In cases in which you have to travel some distance to use the material, it is often cheaper as well as timesaving to arrange for photoduplication. You can generally have the repository make microfilmed or photostatic copies (the former being much less expensive but requiring a special machine for reading) or can secure permission to take photocopies yourself with such a device as a Contura. (The latter can be purchased for a reasonable price from F. G. Ludwig Associates, Pease Road, Woodbridge, Conn.)

3. Dates. The assignment of a date to an historical event may be quite complicated. Earlier dates were related to rulers and dynasties. In more recent times historians have attempted to fit all happenings to the Christian calendar. In 1582 Pope Gregory XIII proclaimed the Gregorian ("New Style," or "N. S.") Calendar, advancing ten days and providing for necessary future adjustments to bring the Julian ("Old Style," or "O. S.") Calendar into conformity with the solar year and fixing 1 January (earlier usually 25 March) as the beginning of the new year. Protestant England resisted the innovation until 1752, by which time it was necessary to advance eleven days. Dates for the intervening period are generally translated into New Style. Washington's Birthday of 11 February 1731 (or 1731/32) , O. S. thus became 22 February 1732, N. S. "Perpetual calendars" are widely available to give you the day of the week if needed. It was not until about 1000 A.D. that dating the year from the presumed birth of Jesus came into general use. Non-Christian civilizations for convenience now generally use the Christian calendar, sometimes employing such euphemisms as "Before the Common Era" (B. C. E.) and "Common Era" (C. E.) .

4 CRITICISM

Of some things I am not sure, but I am sure of one thing: that it is better and more manly to think that we ought to investigate what we do not know than idly to assume that we cannot, or ought not to, investigate. For this I would fight to the limit of my power in word and deed.
Plato, *Socratic Dialogues,* "Meno."

I have often said that the use of a university is to make young gentlemen as unlike their fathers as possible.
Woodrow Wilson, *Public Papers: The New Democracy,*
I, 199.

Your pursuit of evidence will have had much in common with a detective's search for clues. In the evaluation of the evidence which you uncover, you will follow rules of evidence comparable to those of a court of law. An obligation rests upon every historian as it does upon a member of a jury to render a verdict to the best of his ability solely in accordance with the evidence and with as full a sense of his responsibility. The development of the judicial process, although not yet free from the possibility of honest human error, has been the basis for security and freedom in human society. The historian's verdict upon which we base our evaluations of men and institutions of the past in order to see the present in perspective and attempt to prepare for the future can be, everything considered, at least as trustworthy as that of a court empowered to pass sentence on a man's property and life. It is not by chance that tyrants and demagogues seek both to subvert the courts and to pervert history. You will have to weigh conflicting evidence, discount special pleading, and bear in mind the fallibility of human observation and memory. And likewise your decision will be subject to review.

Although absolute truth may be an abstract ideal for human beings, you must never relax in the effort to attain it. If you make a sincere and wholehearted effort, avoiding easy excuses for your failures, you can achieve an objective attitude and approach a usable approximation of the truth.

The basic requirements are simple. Only four questions, each with its subquestions, must be answered:

1. Opportunity? Was the person who is your ultimate source of information in a position to observe the events he recorded? Was he intelligent and observant? Was he an insider? Did he have a background for understanding the event? If he got his information from someone else, all your criteria will have to be repeated for that person.

2. Objectivity?   What sort of reputation did your informant have for honesty as well as intelligence? Was he known in his own circle as an addle-pated gossip who, like Eva the duck in one of James Thurber's "Further Fables for Our Time" (*The New Yorker*, 28 July 1956), "had two mouths but only one ear"? What were his prejudices and involvements of self-interest that must be discounted? As in the courtroom, an admission against self-interest, other things being equal, is most convincing. What sort of feeling do you get from the internal evidence of the record he has left as to his discernment and probity? In time you will tend to acquire, as the result of experience stored up in your subconsciousness, a sort of sixth sense that will alert you to the tell-tale signs of a muddled or dishonest witness.

3. Transmission?   Did your informant set down his observations imme-diately? Did he later rewrite them? Students of military history are familiar with the remark that on the day of battle Truth stands naked, but that as quickly as possible thereafter she begins to wrap herself in the garments of self-justification and myth. After the passage of even a single day a man's memory begins subtly to revise reality to magnify his own wisdom and the righteousness of his cause. Did your man record his information in a spirit of anger, apology, fear, despair, elation, or judicial calmness? To whom did he address himself? Was he writing to a confidant to whom he felt an obligation of candor or to someone whom he was trying to convince? If he spoke or wrote publicly, was his version challenged? Did he employ a "ghost writer"?

4. Meaning?   You must always remain aware of the changing denotation and connotation of words — consulting where necessary dictionaries that indi-cate word meanings at various periods, and avoid pitfalls of irony and figures of speech. Beware of that worst of judicial sins — taking the evidence away from its context. Learn the special vocabularies and slang of different callings and levels of society. As you become saturated in some period of the past, you will be able to feel and think like men and women of that time and yet retain the critical perspective of your own.[10]

---

10. We have not gone into the somewhat artificial distinction between "external" and "internal" evidence and other terms tending toward technical jargon. They are a heritage from German scholars who, influenced by Medieval Scholasticism, placed much emphasis on a categorization that both advanced and to some extent impeded the clarification of history as a scholarly discipline. Most notable of these men was Ernst Bernheim, whose *Lehrbuch der historischen Methode und Geschichtsphilosophie,* first published in 1889, reached a sixth edition at Leipzig in 1908. The French scholars Charles Victor Langlois and Charles Seignobos drew on Bernheim to some extent in their *Introduction aux études historiques* (Paris, 1898), which was translated into English by C. G. Berry and published as *Introduction to the Study of History* (New York: Henry Holt & Co., 1912). See also Louis Reichenthal Gottschalk, Clyde Kluckhohn, and Robert Angell, *The Use of Personal Documents in History, Anthropol-ogy, and Sociology* . . . . Social Science Research Council, *Bulletin 53* (New York: Social Science Research Council, 1945), xiv, 243 pp.

5 | CONSTRUCTION

Yet here, Laertes? Aboard, aboard, for shame!
The wind sits in the shoulder of your sail, and you are stay'd
for.
There; my blessing with thee!
And these few precepts in thy memory see thou character.

Hamlet, Act I, scene 3.

When you have exhaustively collected and carefully evaluated your evidence, you are ready to fit it together into a pattern of reconstructed truth. In this undertaking you will utilize to the full your powers of logical organization, integration, imaginative insight, and scholarly objectivity. You should be able to apply all, or most, of the following suggestions.

A. General

Leaving some of the more technical problems for discussion in later sections of this chapter, we need first to deal with four general procedures:

1. Outline. The primary secret of a well constructed treatise is the fully integrated outline, arranged to trace the progress of your subject chronologically and by component topics and areas. You may find it best to open briefly with some dramatic and revealing event from the middle or end of your story and then turn back to the beginning of the developments that led to it. At the very inception of your research you will rough it out in preliminary form on the basis of your prior information, surmises, and unanswered questions. You will thereafter continually expand, revise, and rearrange it until you have completed the final version of a finished paper that represents the very best efforts of which

CONCLUSION
DISCUSSION
INTRODUCTION

you are capable. Always carry with you a note pad to jot down any sudden inspiration, either in the form of a concept or an illuminating phrase, that may unexpectedly arise out of the fermentation that will be taking place in your subconscious mind.

The general structure of your outline and the research and writing that develop around that outline should be analogous to a fundamental artifact of modern building construction, the steel I-beam that, by replacing the solid wooden beams that once supported each floor of the structure, has made it feasible to erect buildings ten times the height of what was possible by earlier methods. Seen in cross-section, each such beam is broad at the base, as your introduction should be, so that it can rest firmly on the construction that preceded it; then it rises, as should discussion of the central theme of your study, as straightly narrow as possible in order to carry its proper burden without itself becoming cumbersome; and finally it, as will your conclusion, broadens out again to support further construction at the next level.

2. Note filing. In order to use your notes effectively you must be able to find them as you need them.

a. Bibliographical cards. File first in metal boxes, obtainable at any stationery or variety store, that will hold about three hundred entries plus guide cards. As you continue your researches you can invest economically in a cardboard box file or in a double drawered steel filing case that holds some three or four thousand cards. These latter are so designed that they will stack neatly on top of each other, as you acquire additional ones, to accommodate all the bibliographical cards that you are likely to accumulate in a lifetime of historical investigation. For any particular study you will file your cards alphabetically under the appropriate categories indicated in paragraph 5-E-17, below.

b. Content notes. An expanding cardboard file of appropriate size will suffice at first, but you may soon need to purchase a cardboard box file or a stackable double drawered steel file, for which you can also buy a base. If you are filing your notes in folders you will need to get a 6 x 9 inch file to accommodate 5 x 8 inch notes. As your study develops you will file your content notes in tabbed sections (if on cards) or in folders (if on sheets of paper) in accordance with your outline, and refile them as you revise that outline. Finally each tabbed section or folder should represent a section or sub-section of your outline and correspond to a paragraph in your final paper.

3. Oral presentation. Before your research takes its final written form you may be called upon to present an oral report before a class, such as a research seminar, or to deliver a public lecture. The same essential organization should be followed in both oral and written presentation. But a somewhat different literary style is required for the ear than the eye, especially in the need for repetition — preferably by paraphrase — of key items of fact and interpretation that a reader could fix in his mind by re-reading. (On the other hand it may be inadvisable during the course of composition to read your manuscript aloud, since the pauses and inflections of your voice may lend an emphasis and a clarity of meaning that will not be apparent in the cold print.) The most effective oral presentation is usually achieved by speaking informally, after thorough mental rehearsal, from a detailed outline. This outline should contain reference numbers, perhaps in red pencil, which will enable you to pick up without fumbling any of your reference notes that you plan to quote verbatim. If you try to read a formal paper aloud, except to a mature audience of fellow scholars, you are likely to lose contact with your audience. And any venture at talking directly from your notes is likely to degenerate into a rambling discourse. In a seminar you can assist your auditors by giving each member of the class (1) a brief typed outline, (2) a bibliography of your chief sources, and (3) a list of unfamiliar names and terms that you will use — and which you will have checked to insure correct pronunciation. Your classmates, in turn, can help you with their oral comments and, later, with written critiques.

4. Composition. You will construct the rough draft of your treatise paragraph by paragraph, guided by your outline. In writing each paragraph, first read over the notes contained in your folder or tabbed section. Then *close the folder and do not consult it again until you have finished your draft of the paragraph,* going back afterward to verify facts and to pick up overlooked points. If you attempt to work directly from your notes, one at a time, you are likely to produce a scrapbook rather than an original study in which you have distilled a new essence from your material.

Many writers find it best to write their first draft in longhand, continuing as long as their inspiration holds up and then pausing to copy each section on the typewriter, revising to some extent as they do so and inserting footnote references (see 5-D, below, especially the unnumbered third paragraph). Some writers prefer not to insert footnotes until their final draft, instead placing corresponding numbers in the text and on each note to be cited in order to indicate the ultimate location. Type your drafts with double or triple spaces between the lines to leave room for corrections and interpolations. Always make a carbon copy and store it in a separate place as insurance against mishap. To avoid confusion you may wish to identify each draft or revision by some device such as jotting down on the corner of each page the date on which you prepared it. If you strike out a passage and then, after reconsideration, decide to retain it, write *stet* (from the Latin for "let it stand") beside it.

The number of drafts and revisions you will need to make will depend to some extent on the thoroughness with which you have mastered your subject. You may be both sobered and consoled to learn that many gifted and experienced writers have to rewrite again and again before they achieve the clarity and air of spontaneity at which they aim from the beginning.

B. Quotations

Quotations from the original sources or from authors of secondary works can help to point up your narrative if used with discriminating selectivity. (They have already been discussed to some extent in reference to note taking in section 3-2, page 34, above.) They are justified when they provide a special flavor from the original or bear upon some critical point that must be precisely demonstrated. Deletions must never change the original meaning. Indicate the deletion by three alternately spaced dots (thus . . .) if it is within a sentence, or by four if it immediately follows a completed sentence in the original (thus. . . .), the first one being the period belonging to that sentence, or (thus . . . .) if the quotation ends with an uncompleted sentence. Fit short prose quotations, preceded and followed by quotation marks, into your narrative in such a way as to preserve sentence capitalization if it is in the original. In such a case it would be — Captain John Knight replied, "Brave men will not surrender." If not — Captain John Knight replied that "brave men will not surrender." Quotation marks within the original are changed to single quotation marks (and, if absolutely unavoidable, a quotation within that quotation would be given double quotation marks), but otherwise the punctuation, capitalization, and spelling of the original should be followed wherever possible. This generalization would not hold if you were preparing a source book for undergraduates or the general reader. In such a case you would have reasonable leeway in modernization of punctuation and spelling to assist readability. Where you must interpolate an explanatory word or phrase of your own, place it in brackets. Parentheses are assumed to have been in the original. You can interpolate the notation "[*sic*]" in the text to show that the error it immediately follows is contained in the work you are quoting — thus protecting yourself from the assumption that it may be a factual or typographical error of your own.

1. Quotation marks. Note that periods and commas are always placed within the end quotation marks; colons and semicolons outside. Question marks, dashes, and exclamation points stand outside unless they are in the original.

2. Extensive quotations. A quotation of more than three lines should be set apart from your text by indenting it an additional four spaces and typing it single spaced — in contrast to the double spacing of your narrative text. (You will, of course, double space between paragraphs.) Use no quotation marks except as in the original. Indent four more spaces if you start with a paragraph beginning of the original, and do the same for subsequent paragraph beginnings. If the quotation begins within a sentence, do not capitalize the first word (unless, of course, it is a proper noun); and in this case the phrase of the text preceding it should not end with any punctuation mark, but should lead into it in the same manner as has been indicated for shorter quotations. Deletions within the quotation should also follow the same rules. Use common sense in paragraphing within it. Follow that within the original as closely as practical, but do not have broken lines straggling down a page.

In cases in which you are quoting *in extenso* — as, for example, in an appendix or in the compilation of a book of sources — you may run a line of dots, alternately spaced, from margin to margin to indicate the deletion of one or more paragraphs, either at the beginning, within, or at the end of your quotation. This is generally unnecessary in the case of fairly brief quotations in the midst of your text, where it would make for an unattractive appearance. You can, if you wish, indicate that the segments of your quotation are some distance apart in the original by interrupting the quotation with a line or so of text conveying this information. You will, however, need to use such a line of dots to indicate the deletion of one or more lines in the quotation of poetry.

In quoting, you must remember that the copyright holder has full ownership of the writing for twenty-eight years — fifty-six if he renews the copyright. It is advisable to secure his permission before including a quotation of any line of verse, particularly of copyrighted popular songs, or more than five lines of prose in any work you intend for publication. (If his address is unknown to you, it can be obtained from the publisher, who, indeed, will often obtain the consent for you if you explain the use you wish to make of it.) Consent is not needed for the use of brief necessary quotations for purposes of rejoinder or in the writing of a book review, in which cases the courts assume "fair use" (Copyright Office, Library of Congress, circulars No. 20, 22, 91).

3. Foreign words. Quotations from foreign languages should, as a rule, be put into English that will as far as possible preserve the overtones as well as the literal meaning of the original. (See, for example, James Gauchez Anderson, *Le Mot Juste: A Dictionary of English and French Homonyms.* New York: E. P. Dutton & Co., c. 1938.) Short idiomatic phrases or terms of particular importance may be quoted in the original language if their meaning is explained. Do not give in to the temptation to flaunt your knowledge of Urdu or Chagatay; it will be sufficiently demonstrated by your references. When foreign words or phrases are set in a context of English, they should be underscored (italicized in a printed work) unless they are enclosed in quotation marks. This does not, of course, apply to names of people or places or to expressions which have become sufficiently anglicized as to be generally understood; in which case foreign accent markings are often not used. (When in doubt consult *Webster's Dictionary,* in which parallel bars in the margin or similar marks indicate the need for italicization.)

C. Bibliographical Form

Reference has already been made in section 3-1, above, to the making out of bibliographical cards; and in section 5-E-17, below, the location of the bibliography in your completed paper is indicated.

There is no universally followed form for bibliographical entries. It would be all but impossible to prepare examples to cover every possible contingency. Two simple governing rules should be kept in mind: (1) the form used should be such as to enable anyone to look up the item cited with a minimum of difficulty and offer him a maximum of pertinent information consistent with brevity, and (2) any form and its necessary variations should be simple, logical, and consistent. Differences between the forms used for bibliographical items and footnote references should be the very minimum required by their differences in function. The following examples should enable anyone who keeps these principles in mind to adapt these forms to any unusual titles.[11]

1. Books.

The data following the date of publication below are not included in most systems, but are suggested here because of their usefulness to the reader. The example of annotation for an obviously fictitious title — as are most of those that follow — will not herein be repeated for subsequent items. Words underscored in typing are italicized in print. A double line of underscoring would

---

11. Many helpful suggestions can be obtained from any of the following: Kate L. Turabian, *A Manual for Writers of Term Papers, Theses, and Dissertations* (Rev. ed.; Chicago: University of Chicago Press, c. 1955), v, 82 pp.; William Riley Parker, "The MLA Style Sheet," *PMLA,* LXVI (Apr. 1951), 3-31 (also obtainable in separate form from 100 Washington Square East, New York 3); Griffith Thompson Pugh, *Guide to Research Writing* (Boston, etc.: Houghton Mifflin Co., c. 1955), 64 pp.; William Giles Campbell, *Form and Style in Thesis Writing* (*Ibid.,* c. 1954), 114 pp.; Lucyle Hook and Mary Virginia Gaver, *The Research Paper* (2d ed.; New York: Prentice-Hall, Inc., 1952), 85 pp.; the volumes by Bauer, Hockett, and Kent referred to in footnote 8, above; and Oscar Handlin, *et al., Harvard Guide to American History* (Cambridge, Mass.: Belknap Press of Harvard University, 1954), pp. 38-44. In adhering to the principles stated above it has been necessary in the present booklet, after the most careful thought, to vary somewhat from the forms recommended by any one of them, as they do from each other. Clarence Edwin Carter, *Historical Editing* (National Archives, *Bulletin No. 7*), indispensable for its special purpose, represents decades of experience in the publication of official documents.

> Knight, John, <u>The</u> <u>History</u> <u>of</u> <u>Exploration</u>
> <u>in</u> <u>America</u>. New York: Brown Co., 1927. xi,
> 693 pp. Illus., maps, bibl., appdcs., index.
>
> Awarded the Marco Polo prize. An exhaus-
> tive, unbiased treatment, based on research
> in principal European and North and South
> American archives. Propounds thesis that the
> spirit of adventure and the quest for econ-
> omic advantage were equally essential in the
> opening up of the New World.

indicate words to be set in small capital letters, and triple underscoring indicates full capitals. Sometimes, following the form used in the book you are listing, the pagination might run — xi, 693, x pp., or 11, 693, 10 pp.

a. **Variations in authorship.** To aid your reader to find the book as conveniently as possible, give the author's full name, if ascertainable, regardless of how it may appear on the title page. Catalogue cards, printed by the Library of Congress and used by most other libraries, usually contain this information. To avoid confusion concerning authors of identical names you may indicate their dates of birth — Knight, John (b. 1883) or (1883-1948) or include an appropriate explanation in your bibliography and first footnote references.

(1) *Do not use titles or suffixes* (Prof., Gen., Dr., Msgr., Ph.D., S.J., etc.) unless to prevent confusion through lack of needed information — Knight, Mrs. John; or MacAnridire, Sister John the Baptist — but Knight, Jane (Squire); or MacAnridire, Mary Magdalen. A nobleman may properly be listed under his title — Herrenburg, Jakob Karl Junker, 8th Baron von.

(2) *If no author's name is given* on the title page but it can be ascertained from other sources, enclose it in brackets. A pseudonym should be preceded by the real name in brackets — [Knight, John] Gaylord Chevalier — and alphabetized under it. If the author is unknown, list alphabetically under the first word of the title after the article (a, an, the), if any.

(3) *Multiple authors.* Two authors — Knight, John, and James Charles Squire, <u>The History</u> . . . . Since the item will be filed and listed under the name of the first author given, there is no need to reverse the normal order for other names. Three authors — Knight, John, James Charles Squire, and George D. Page. The assumption here is that Knight has no ascertainable middle name and that it has been possible to discover only the middle initial for Page. Four or more authors — Knight, John, <u>et al</u>., <u>The History</u> . . . . Even if the authors should be related, each will be given his full name — Knight, John, and Jane (Squire) Knight.

(4) *Organization as author.*

Middle States Historical Association, <u>Annual</u> <u>Report</u> <u>for</u> <u>the</u> <u>Year</u> <u>1955</u>. Crossways, Del.: Nonesuch Publishers, 1956. 213 pp. Index.

(5) *Editorship.* If a book consists of the work of a number of authors working under one or more editors, or is an edited source work, it appears under the editor's name in the same manner as if author —   Knight, John, ed., <u>The</u> <u>History</u> . . . . — Knight, John, and James Charles Squire, eds., <u>The</u> <u>History</u> . . . .

(6) *Translators' names follow the title.*

Ritter, Johann, <u>The</u> <u>History</u> <u>of</u> <u>Exploration</u> <u>in</u> <u>America</u>, trans. [or — trans., with notes,] James Charles Squire. New York: Brown Co., 1927. xxi, 963 pp. Maps, bibl., index.

b. Variations in title.

(1) *In Romance languages, Swedish,* and *Russian* only proper nouns and the first word of the title and subtitle are capitalized. French authors sometimes exercise an option to capitalize other significant words.

Chevalier, Jean, <u>Histoire</u> <u>de</u> <u>l'exploration</u> <u>en</u> <u>Amerique</u>.

(2) *In German, Dutch, Danish,* and *Polish* the first word of the title and subtitle and all nouns and words used as nouns (plus, in Dutch, adjectives derived from proper nouns and, in German, adjectives derived from the names of persons) are capitalized. In *Latin* all proper nouns and adjectives derived therefrom are capitalized.

Ritter, Johann, <u>Geschichte</u> <u>der</u> <u>Erforschung</u> <u>in</u> <u>Amerika</u>.

An alternative system, especially desirable for words adapted from other alphabets, is to use the English system of capitalization for all foreign book titles.

(3) *Titles in languages generally unfamiliar* should be followed by an English translation in brackets.

Bogatyr, Ivan, <u>Istoriia</u> <u>issledovania</u> <u>v</u> <u>Amerike</u> [The history of exploration in America].

(4) *Sub-titles* are treated in the same fashion as titles.

Knight, John, <u>The</u> <u>History</u> <u>of</u> <u>Exploration</u> <u>in</u> <u>America</u>: <u>An</u> <u>Adventure</u> <u>during</u> <u>Four</u> <u>Centuries</u>.

You are not bound by the punctuation you find on the title page, but should follow a standard system.

(5) *Volume in a series.*

Knight, John, <u>The</u> <u>History</u> <u>of</u> <u>Exploration</u> <u>in</u> <u>America</u>, Vol. IV of <u>The</u> <u>Saga</u> <u>of</u> <u>Mankind</u>, ed. James Charles Squire. New York: Brown Co., 1927.

xi, 693 pp. Illus., maps, bibl., appdcs., index. Part of a series that is an integrated work.

Knight, John, The History of Exploration in America. Studies in History Edited by the Faculty of the Graduate School of the Central University of America, Vol. XXXI, No. 3. Centralia, Mo.: Central University of America Press, 1927. xi, 693 pp. Illus., maps, bibl., appdcs., index. For a volume in an indefinite series.

Sometimes publishers carry a half-title page, preceding the title page, or may carry it at the top of the title page, bearing a rather general title such as "Brown Studies in History." In most cases it is not necessary to indicate this on your bibliographical card.

c. Variations in publishing data.

(1) *Subsequent editions.*

Knight, John, The History of Exploration in America. Rev. ed.; New York: Brown Co., 1934. xxii, 693 pp. Maps, bibl., index. or

Knight, John, The History of Exploration in America. 2d ed., rev. and enl.; New York: Brown Co., 1934. xxii, 739 pp. Bibl., index.

(2) *Multiple volumes.*

Knight, John, The History of Exploration in America. 2d ed; 6 vols.; New York: Brown Co., 1925-28. Illus., maps, bibl. No pages are, as a rule, needed for multiple volumes, since substantial size is suggested.

(3) *Place of publication.*

If the publisher maintains major offices in two cities, they may be indicated in this fashion — New York & San Francisco: Brown Co., 1927. If three or more are listed, select the first or the one most featured — New York, etc.: Brown Co., 1927. If place of publication is not indicated but is known from other sources — [New York:] Brown Co., 1927. If it is unknown — n. p., — for "no place" — Ocre Co., 1927.

There appears to be a growing disposition to regard the indication of place of publication (which once suggested the likelihood of national or regional bias) for university presses and the better known modern commercial publishers in the United States as superfluous, but its deletion has not yet become general.

(4) *Publisher's designation.* The practice of giving the name of the publisher (in earlier times often simply a job printer) although still not universal, is now widespread and in many cases is beyond argument, especially in more recent publications. The imprint of a respected publishing house or university press tends, with occasional lapses, to carry an assumption of responsibility, while that of certain others should alert the experienced reader to be on guard against special pleading.

If "The Brown Company" were differently styled it might be one of the following — Brown Bros. Co.; Z. Brown & Sons Co., Ltd. (Ltd. usually indicates a corporation in the British Commonwealth) ; or Brown & Green.

If the publisher is not given but is known from other sources, place in brackets. If unknown — New York: privately printed, 1927.

(5) *Date of publication.*

If no date of publication is given, use copyright date on the back of the title page — New York: Brown Co, c. 1927. If neither is given but is known from other sources, place in brackets. If both are unknown — New York: Brown Co., n.d. — for "no date."

2. Public documents. The following examples are not fictitious.

U. S. Senate, 76th Cong., 1st Sess., Committee on Education and Labor, Violations of Free Speech and Rights of Labor, Senate Report 6, pt. 3, Industrial Munitions. Washington: Government Printing Office, 1939. iv, 240 pp. Illus., appdcs., index.

U. S. House of Representatives, 81st Cong., 1st Sess., Committee on Agriculture, Hearings . . . General Farm Problem, pt. 2, April 7, 11, 12, 25, 26, 1949 (Serial P). Washington: Government Printing Office, 1949. iii, 187-357 pp.

U. S., Register of Debates in Congress . . . [1824-37]. 14 vols. in 29; Washington: Gales & Seaton, 1825-37.

U. S. Congress, The Congressional Globe . . . . 46 vols. in 111; Washington: Globe Office, 1834-73.

Great Britain, Parliament, House of Commons, Joint Committee on Indian Constitutional Reform, Report . . . together with the Proceedings of the Committee, House of Commons Reports and Papers, 1932-1933, No. 112. 6 vols.; London: H. M. Stationery Office, 1934.

League of Nations, Mixed Committee on the Problem of Nutrition, Final Report . . . on the Relation of Nutrition to Health, Agriculture, and Economic Policy (A.13.1937.II.A). Geneva, 1937. 327 pp.

United Nations, General Assembly, Annual Report of the Secretary-General on the Work of the Organization, 1 July 1951-30 June 1952 (A/2141). New York, 1952.

3. Articles and essays.

Knight, John, "Matchless Magellan: The Story of a Voyage," The Middle States Historical Journal, XXXII (Apr. 1927), 508-27.

Or, if no month or season is given — XXXII, No. 3 (1927).There is no need to give the subtitle, if any, of a well known periodical.

Knight, John, "Ferdinand Magellan," pp. 347-79 in The Great Explorers, ed. James Charles Squire. New York: Brown Co., 1927.

Knight, John, "Ferdinand Magellan," pp. 347-79 in The Spanish Adventurers, ed. James Charles Squire, Vol. IV of The Saga of Mankind, ed. George D. Page. New York: Brown Co., 1927.

Knight, John, "Columbus, Christopher," Special Encyclopedia, II, 200-205, ed. James Charles Squire. Prairie City, Mo.: Pink & White, Inc., 1923.

Knight, John, "Vasco da Gama," General Encyclopaedia, 12th ed.; XXXI, 311-15. No other publication data are needed for a well known encyclopedia.

4. Book reviews.

Page, George D., Review of The History of Exploration in America, by John Knight, The Middle States Historical Journal, XXXIII (Apr. 1928), 400-402.

5. Unpublished studies.

Page, George Dogberry, Jr., "London Sailors under Henry VIII: A Study of Their Origins." Unpublished Ph.D. dissertation [or MS M. A. thesis], Central University of America, 1955. ix, 139 pp.

6. Newspapers.

The Prairie City (Missouri) Cyclone.

Expresses the views of the editor and publisher, John Ritter, an uncompromising Greenbacker who opposed even a silver supported currency. Declining advertisements by merchants suggest economic pressure against him.

The (London) Times, 1 June 1892-30 Nov. 1893.

The New York Times, 1 June-30 Nov. 1892.

The [Prairie City, Missouri] Farmer's Friend.

If the place of publication is not included in the title but is given elsewhere in the newspaper, enclose it in parentheses; if it has to be determined by additional research, place it in brackets. If your investigation covers many newspapers, it may be convenient for you to group them by areas in your bibliography. In this case you may not need to insert the place of publication in the title.

7. Manuscript collections.

Knight, John, MSS. Library of Congress. 27 boxes, approximately 12,000 letters, 1871-1905, 2 letter press books, 1884-87, and diary, 1901-1902.

Important for picture of student and professorial life of period. Unfortunately the correspondence relating to Professor Knight's quarrel with President George Knabe of Midwest College appears to have been removed, and probably destroyed, before the collection was deposited in the Library of Congress.

Squire, James Charles, MSS Diary, 19 Mar. 1905-17 Feb. 1943. Central University of America Library. 38 vols. Used by permission of Mrs. James Charles Squire.

State, Department of, Consular Dispatches, Manila. National Archives. 13 vols., 1817-99.

State, Department of, Decimal File 862.00, 1910-29. National Archives.

Navy Department, Area 9 File, Record Group 45. National Archives.

Consult the repository in which the collection is located concerning the type of identification that will enable anyone to go immediately to it. (See page 50, 5-D-7, final paragraph, below.)

8. Personal correspondence.

Knight, John, 6 letters, Feb.-Apr. 1956, to the author.

9. Oral interviews.

Knight, John, personal interview, New York, 19 Mar. 1956, with the author.

James C. Squire Manufacturing Co., Prairie City, Missouri. Personal interview with James Charles Squire, Jr., President, at Widget Manufacturers of America National Convention, Chicago, 3 Oct. 1956.

D. Footnotes

Footnotes are of three types, although they appear together without distinction. They are: (1) Explanatory notes, consisting of comments or the discussion of somewhat digressive matters which you feel it necessary to deal with without unnecessarily impeding the flow of your main treatment. These should be used sparingly. In general, if a subject can not be fitted smoothly into your narrative, it is better to omit it altogether. There are few things more annoying than attempting to follow the course of a thin stream of narrative through a morass of explanatory footnotes. In the hands of a skilled writer footnote comments can sometimes be used to spice the narrative. A prime example is Robert L. Duffus, *The Innocents at Cedro,* in which humorous asides add measurably to the book's nostalgic charm. (2) Cross references to other parts of your narrative or to other footnotes are useful devices wherever it is necessary to treat different aspects of the same topic at two or more points in the development of your subject. (But try not to put your reader in the position where he is incessantly having to turn back and forth.) You can often fit such notes into your text, itself, enclosed in parentheses. (3) Every direct quotation, each statement of fact that is not generally known or self-evident, and any interpretation borrowed from another source *must* be indicated in some fashion. This is by far the most necessary function of footnotes, enabling the reader to check the accuracy and justification of anything whatsoever that you include in your treatise. A footnote number should appear in your text immediately following the statement that you must vouch for, even if in the midst of a sentence, and should be raised one-half space. If all the matter in a paragraph or longer section is derived from the same source or sources, one footnote will often suffice for the whole. Footnotes should be numbered consecutively for each chapter, or for the entire paper if it is a short one, rather than starting afresh with each page. Even in the case of reference citations it is often possible to indicate your source in the body of the text, even strengthening the latter thereby, setting off the specific page or pages referred to by the use of commas or parentheses.

Footnotes are normally grouped at the bottom of the page preceded by the appropriate number (often raised one-half space) , and separated from the text by a solid line of type from margin to margin. For a textbook they might be cited at the end of a chapter, and for a book intended for the general public at the back of the book — especially if they are very extensive. (See p. 54, 5-E-15, below.) They should be single spaced, in contrast to your text which would be double spaced; but with double spacing between the footnote paragraphs. If the numbered references are brief, two or more may be put on the same line. When the material in your text is derived from several sources that cannot readily be separated from each other in proper sequence, you may group them all in one footnote, separated by semicolons. A long footnote may, if necessary, be completed at the bottom of the next page before the next footnote, if there is one there.

In all but your final draft, however, it is advisable to place the footnote on the next line immediately following the portion of the text to which it refers, drawing lines from margin to margin both before and after the footnote to separate it from the text. In this case it is best to type it double spaced to facilitate corrections. A blank space should be left for the appropriate number in both the text and note so that you can conveniently insert the numbers in your final draft. (See page 39, 5-A-4, second paragraph, above.)

In form, footnote references differ in four respects from bibliographical references: (1) you give the author's name in its regular order, since it will not be filed or listed alphabetically; (2) you place the publishing data in parentheses in order to avoid any confusion with the citation of page numbers; (3) you cite the specific page, or pages, from which the note is taken; and (4) you omit all of the supplemental information indicated after the date of publication in the bibliographical reference. In citing the derivation of your information for the first time in each chapter (as well as in the headings for your content notes) follow the models set forth below.

1. Books.

John Knight, The History of Exploration in America (New York: Brown Co., 1927), p. 7. — or pp. 70-77, 71-72, 703-707, 708-15, 797-811; or i-iii; or I, 7; or Ch. V.

Johann Ritter, The History of Exploration in America, trans. James Charles Squire (3d ed.; New York: Brown Co., 1927), 1, 7.

The presence of a volume number may be considered as making the inclusion of the abbreviation for page unnecessary.

John Knight, The History of Exploration in America: An Adventure during Four Centuries, Vol. IV of The Saga of Mankind, ed. James Charles Squire (New York: Brown Co., 1927), pp. 52-57.

Johannes Knyghte, Historie of New Worlde Exploration (London, 1621), p. 37, in [or — quoted in] James Charles Squire, The Age of Discovery (New York: Brown Co., 1928), p. 101. When the original is not available to you.

If the author and title, or any other parts of the necessary information, are given in the text they need not be repeated in the footnote. Thus

(New York: Brown Co., 1927), p. 7.

2. Public documents.

U. S. Senate, 76th Cong., 1st Sess., Committee on Education and Labor, Violations of Free Speech and Rights of Labor, Senate Report 6, pt. 3, Industrial Munitions (Washington: Government Printing Office, 1939), pp. 107-15.

U. S. War Department, The War of the Rebellion: A Compilation of the Official Records of the Union and Confederate Armies (hereinafter referred to as O. R.), Ser. I, Vol. XLI, pt. 2 (Washington: Government Printing Office, 1892), p. 455, Maj. Gen. William Starke Rosecrans, Commanding, Department of Missouri, St. Louis, 29 July 1864, to Governor Richard Yates, Springfield, Illinois.

3. Articles and essays.

John Knight, "Matchless Magellan: The Story of a Voyage," The Middle States Historical Journal, XXXII (Apr. 1927), 510.

4. Book reviews.

George D. Page, Review of The History of Exploration in America, by John Knight, The Middle States Historical Journal, XXXIII (Apr. 1928), 401.

5. Unpublished studies.

George Dogberry Page, Jr., "London Sailors under Henry VIII: A Study of Their Origins" (unpublished [or MS] Ph.D. dissertation, Central University of America, 1955), p. 92.

6. Newspapers.

The New York Times, 19 Mar. 1956, pp. 1, 4. [Or C-14, or VI-7.]

The Prairie City (Missouri) Cyclone, 28 Feb. 1958, p. 3. It is general practice not to give page references for small newspapers, but it is a timesaving convenience to the reader that requires little extra effort by the author.

7. Manuscript collections.

Because the reader's interest will be concentrated upon a particular item instead of a collection as a whole, the footnote citation for a manuscript is given in substantially reverse order of the form employed in listing a manuscript collection in your bibliography.

James Charles Squire, New York, 19 Mar. 1897, letter to John Knight, Prairie City, Missouri, File Box 17, John Knight MSS, Library of Congress.

Entry of 13 Aug. 1927, James Charles Squire MS Diary, Vol. 22, Central University of America Library.

Consul Alexander R. Webb, 26 July 1891, to Assistant Secretary Wharton, Consular Dispatches, Manila, Vol. 12, Department of State, National Archives. Titles, place, and date may be omitted if made clear by the text. Since the number of boxes or volumes of collections in public repositories often runs to over one hundred, it is, for consistency, generally advisable to employ Arabic numerals throughout.

Ambassador William E. Dodd, Berlin, 4 Nov. 1933, to Secretary Hull, 862.00/3131, Department of State, National Archives.

Secretary Welles, Washington, 3 Aug. 1865, telegram to Rear Admiral Pearson, Area 9 File, Record Group 45, Navy Department, National Archives.

Minister Henry Lane Wilson, 9 July 1898, to Secretary Day (received 12 Aug.), Dispatches, Chile, Vol. 46, Department of State, National Archives.

Transcribed long distance telephone conversation between Commander Clover and Charles R. Flint, 3 p.m., Wed., 30 Mar. 1898, envelope "AY -- Purchase of Vessels for the Use of the U. S. Navy, 1898," Record Group 45, Navy Department, National Archives.

Consult the repository for the matter to be included in your reference which will enable your reader to go with the greatest possible convenience to the precise letter or document you cite. See, for example, *Information for Searchers Citing Records in the National Archives* (Washington: National Archives, 1957), 4 pp.

8. Personal correspondence.

John Knight, New York, letter, 19 Mar. 1956, to the author.

9. Oral interviews.

James Charles Squire, Jr., President, James C. Squire Manufacturing Co., Prairie City, Missouri, personal interview with the author at Widget Manufacturers of America National Convention, Chicago, 3 Oct. 1956.

10. Classical references.

As a general rule you will cite materials in this field in the forms previously suggested; but since most surviving Classical and Medieval sources are well known to specialists in those fields, it is common practice to refer to them by conventionalized contractions. (See *American Journal of Archaeology,* LIV (July 1950), 268-72, LVI (Jan. 1952), 1-7.) The numerals in the examples below indicate divisions and subdivisions of the work cited in descending order in accordance with its particular arrangement: book, chapter, section, paragraph, verse, sentence, or line.

Pliny Nat. hist. 5.1.12.

Galen De anat. adminst. (Kuhn) 2.217, 224-25. Indicates edition.

Lactanius Divin. instit. 5.2-3.

Appian Mith. 8.

Isaiah 29.21. Where only a single work by an author survives, it is not necessary to give the title. Theological writers commonly use colons between the numbers.

Herod. 2.102. Even the names of particularly familiar authors may be abbreviated.

11. Legal citations.

For the complexities in this field it is advisable to consult *A Uniform System of Citation: Form of Citation and Abbreviations.* 9th ed.; Cambridge, Mass.: Harvard Law Review, 1955. iv, 92 pp. Index. Price $0.50.

Most commonly cited in this special manner by the general historian would be court decisions, as

Dartmouth College v. Woodward, 4 Wheaton 518 (1819).
which identifies a decision of the Supreme Court of the United States by reference to the plaintiff and defendant, the volume, the report editor (a practice abandoned in 1875), page, and date.

Case of S. S. "Wimbledon," Permanent Court of International Justice (commonly and hereinafter as P. C. I. J.), Ser. A., No. 1 (1923), pp. 23-28.

12. Additional citations in a chapter.

After you have cited a book or other reference by its full title and publishing information in accordance with the appropriate form shown above, you will thereafter refer to it throughout a chapter or short paper in a briefer form. Recent practice is increasingly toward using a "short form," thus:

Knight, History of Exploration, p. 7.

Knight, "Matchless Magellan," pp. 511-12.

Squire, London, 3 Oct. 1897, to Knight, Prairie City, Knight MSS.

The short form (which must be used anyway in those instances where one has included two or more works by the same author) has the additional advantage of making it easier for the reader to recall the work as previously cited. Where there are two or more authors with the same given name, they will be additionally identified by their first names or initials. Titles that are awkward to abbreviate may be given some rather arbitrary designation, with a note appended to the first citation, such as — (hereinafter referred to as Sen. Rept. 6) — for the first citation contained in 5-D-2, above.

The Latin form, using abbreviations, is, however, still widely used. Its advantage is its brevity. It would be as follows:

Knight, op. cit., p. 7.

Or, if one is referring to precisely the same pages as before, including an entire article or essay, he might use the form

Knight, loc. cit.

These are abbreviations, respectively, of *opere citato* (in the work cited) and *loco citato* (in the place cited).

There is one Latin form, from *ibidem,* meaning "the same," that will probably continue to be used for its convenience when citing a work again *immediately* after it has been referred to in the previous footnote:

Ibid.   Means not only the same title but same pages.
Ibid., pp. 101-107.   Means same title but different pages.

Other frequently encountered abbreviations and Latin words, of which most of those in Latin are now often used in the form of their English equivalents, are:

c.	(copyright)
ca.	(*circa* — at or near a given date)
cf.	(*confer* — compare with or consult)
e. g.	(*exempli gratia* — for example)
et al.	(*et alii* — and others)
et seq.	(*et sequens* — and following)
ff.	(pages following)
i. e.	(*id est* — that is)
infra	(below, later on in the text)

MS	(one manuscript, or used as adjective)
MSS	(more than one manuscript, usually a collection, as — John Knight MSS, Library of Congress)
n.	(note)
passim	(here and there)
q. v.	(*quod vide* — which see)
sic	(thus — to show that a statement is correctly quoted, although original is erroneous)
supra	(above — earlier in the text)
vide	(see)

E. Final Arrangement

A published book might conceivably include all of the following, and perhaps still other parts; but your own work, if it is a term paper or thesis, will probably contain only those items preceded by asterisks. Those preceded by two asterisks are essential. Articles in periodicals may in some degree informally reflect much the same general order.

★1. **Blank page.**

2. **Half title.**

3. **Series title.**

★★4. **Title page.** Each line on this page should be equally balanced on each side of an imaginary perpendicular line down the middle of the page. First comes your title and your subtitle, if any, without a period at the end. If the subtitle is placed on a second line, there is no punctuation after the title. Half way down the page comes your full name, preceded by "by" and followed, if a thesis or dissertation, by your previous degree (s) , together with granting institution and year of award. You will indicate at the bottom of the page the course for which it is a term paper, or if a thesis the institution, degree, and date thereof as stipulated by the practices of the college in which you are enrolled. For example,

LONDON SAILORS UNDER HENRY VIII

A STUDY OF THEIR ORIGINS

by

George Dogberry Page, Jr.
A. B., 1954, Midwest College

A thesis submitted to the Graduate Faculty of Arts and Letters of the Central University of America in partial satisfaction of the requirements for the degree of Master of Arts in History.

June 1955

Thesis directed by John Knight, Ph. D.

or whatever other form may be required by your institution.

If it were a published book, the material following the name of the author might be simply

New York
Brown Co., Inc.
1927

5. Copyright information.

6. Dedication. To be brief and dignified, without either cloying sentimentality or ingratiating flattery, if used at all.

7. Preface. A vestige of the old "apology" by the author, it can be used briefly either by the author, the editor of the series if the work is a volume in such a series, or some other person to state the circumstances that led to the undertaking and the limitations that have necessarily been placed upon its scope. Its import may very well be carried over to the Introduction (5-E-13, below.)

8. Acknowledgments. These should include only those persons and institutions who have given you substantial assistance, and generally in order of the value of their aid, not of their standing in the profession. Never use them to imply that your work enjoys impressive sponsorship. They may be included in the Preface (5-E-7, above) or as an appendix (5-E-16, below). Don't forget the librarian or archivist who has helped you locate material.

★★**9. Table of contents.** May be either of two types:
    a. Chapter titles, perhaps in shortened form.
    b. Chapter titles, plus list of topics covered in each. Usually found in textbooks. That used in this booklet is, because of its intended use, a particularly elaborate form which also serves in lieu of an index.

★**10. List of maps.**

★**11. List of illustrations.**

★**12. List of charts and tables.**

★**13. Introduction.** In it you indicate the setting of your study, your objectives, and the materials and techniques you have employed. It may constitute the opening section of your first chapter instead of being set apart.

★★**14. The text,** by chapters. With footnotes at bottom of appropriate pages.

15. Reference notes. Employed where the exigencies of publication, usually for a more general audience, require segregation at the end of the volume of the citations that would otherwise be given in footnotes. In this case be sure to give both the chapter number and title at the beginning of each section. It is a further convenience to your reader if you place the page numbers in the text to which the notes refer at the top of each page of reference notes.

★16. **Appendix or appendices,** if any. Here you may reproduce some vital source material to which the reader would not otherwise have access. You may also include what are, in effect, short subordinate essays on related matters that are too specialized for adequate treatment in the body of the text and too lengthy for convenient inclusion in a footnote.

★★17. **Annotated bibliography.** The appropriate forms, including a suggestion for the type of annotative comments you should include, are given in 5-C, above. Works of lesser importance to your study may be described in a word or brief phrase. All items should be listed alphabetically, according to the author's last name, or, if there is no author or editor, by the first word of the title (except a, an, or the, or the equivalent in a foreign language), arranged under something like the following headings. If there are few items in any section, it may be consolidated with some other appropriate section; but sources and secondary works should generally be separated.

a. **Sources.**

(1) *Manuscripts,* personal correspondence, and oral interviews.

(2) Published *public documents.*

(3) *Newspapers.* If very numerous may be sub-divided by nations, states, cities, or political affiliations. Frequently it may be desirable to indicate the period or issues consulted.

(4) *Books, articles,* book reviews, and unpublished studies that are classifiable as sources. Sources, or primary materials, are those that for the particular study in which you are engaged provide ear- and eye-witness accounts or the nearest approximation thereto that you can obtain. The line between sources and secondary works must be drawn functionally for each investigation. For example, William E. Dodd's biography, *Woodrow Wilson and His Work,* would be a primary source for a study of Professor Dodd as an historian, but a secondary work for a study of President Wilson. A primary source (which may simply be called a source) does *not* receive its classification from the fact that it was of primary importance or helpfulness in your study, nor is a secondary work necessarily one that was peripheral to your undertaking. This is emphasized as a common misunderstanding among beginners.

b. **Secondary works.** These will in most cases also consist of books, articles, book reviews, unpublished dissertations, etc. They will generally be listed together, whether published or unpublished, in alphabetical order without sub-division.

18. **Index.** This can be prepared quite easily by using the page proof of a book, starting with the first page and making out a 3 x 5, 4 x 6, or 5 x 8 inch card for each person, event, or topic of importance that you have touched upon. Keep in alphabetical order in a file box, and record the page number each time the name or topic appears. Larger items may be broken into sub-headings.

6 COMMUNICATION

It takes two to speak the truth —
one to speak, and another to hear.
Thoreau, *A Week on the Concord and*
Merrimac Rivers, "Wednesday."

You have undoubtedly experienced both difficulty and compensating satisfaction as you have searched out and digested the material of your investigation. Now, as you set about communicating the significance of your discoveries to someone else, these feelings will reach their climax. Your research that began with a methodology that was essentially scientific will now rise to the level of an art.

1. Elements of style.

a. Words. A good dictionary or thesaurus will aid you in phrasing the exact meaning you wish to convey and in finding synonyms for overworked expressions. A fresh direction of approach to your line of thought may help you to eliminate clichés; and a walk about the room or a stroll around the block is sometimes the best way of finding the precise expression that fits your thought. If you must break a word at the end of a line, follow proper syllabification — taking particular care in the case of proper names. Never leave a single letter from a word standing alone.

b. Sentences. Short, simple, declarative sentences that are predominantly in the active voice — but sufficiently varied to avoid monotony — should be the work horses of your narration. Use adjectives sparingly, adverbs scarcely less so, and only when you are confident that they will stimulate rather than becloud the reader's imagination. Narration takes precedence over description, and both over prolonged commentary. You can normally gain in clarity by bringing as closely together as possible adjectives and the nouns which they describe, adverbs and the verbs they modify, and qualifying phrases or clauses and the things to which they relate. An occasional balanced sentence can, where appropriate, provide a touch of classical dignity, or an inverted one lead the way to a climax. Standard rules of punctuation serve, through habituated usage, as directional signs that help the reader to follow the nuances of your meaning. Often, however, you must exercise a choice as to whether a comma, dash, semicolon, or a period — each of them able to check the eye of the reader as an inflection of the voice or a pause does for the ear — best serves your purpose at any given point.[12] The skilled and experienced writer can make his own exceptions to the rules. There is a military adage that "a good general does not place his army with its back to a river, unless he is of a mind to do so." The sig-

---

12. Useful references concerning matters of grammatical construction include Turabian, *Manual* (see footnote 11, above) and Edwin Campbell Woolley, Franklin W. Scott, and Frederick Bracher, *College Handbook of Composition* (6th ed., rev.; Boston, etc.: D. C. Heath & Co., c. 1958), 474 pp. Henry Watson Fowler, *A Dictionary of Modern English Usage* (Oxford:

nificant word here is "mind," indicating that there should be a good reason for an action contrary to accepted practice. But the beginner should be wary of incautious experimentation.

    c. Paragraphs. In opening a paragraph, a topic sentence should serve as a bridge from the preceding paragraph — sometimes by echoing a key word or concept — and should announce the essence of what is to follow. The rest of the paragraph should then prove the thesis of the opening statement. The concluding sentence should be a summary or comment that serves as an approach to the next bridge. Occasionally it may offer a flourish or peroration on a rising note to drive home an idea. The opening and closing chapters of a book, together with the first and last paragraphs of each of the other chapters and the topic and concluding sentences of each of the other paragraphs — all in their proper sequence — should, ideally, state the essence of the book in intelligible form. Use properly documented quotations where they will be most apt. Exercise the strictest economy of expression that will suffice to convey your full meaning. It is axiomatic that the more thoroughly you have mastered your subject, the more succinctly you can express it. Figures of speech and flecks of color can tone up a narrative; but immoderate indulgence arouses a distaste comparable to that of a banquet consisting entirely of pastries. Revision and rewriting consist largely of excision and condensation while, at the same time, bringing out the deeper meanings and larger implications of your subject. When you doubt the need for any word, phrase, or paragraph, eliminate it.

    d. Chapters. Each chapter, like an article in a periodical, is a miniature book. At the same time it must advance the message of the book as a whole.

    e. Special nomenclature. Be sure to follow accepted forms for such titles as "Reverend" and "Honorable" (or their abbreviations "Rev." and "Hon.") which are always preceded by the word "the," followed by a secondary title thus — the Rev. Mr. (or Dr., or John) Knight. Ascertain the correct form of address for the higher clergy of any church. Present day naval practice is invariably to *omit* the word "the" before ships' names. There is a standard form of reference, often abbreviated, for military units — Co. A, 2d Bn., 136th Arty. Regt., 29th Inf. Div., V Corps, First Army, or First U. S. Army. Underscore (in print italicized) names of plays and set the names of characters therein in quotation marks. Do not confuse the old symbol (known as a "thorn") for "th" with the letter "y." The old English "ye" is the modern "you"; but the practice of early printers of using the letter "y" as a substitute for the thorn has led to confusion. Distinguish between a title of nobility — John, Lord Knightsbridge,

---

Clarendon Press, 1926), Margaret Nicholson, *A Dictionary of American-English Usage Based on Fowler's Modern English Usage* (New York: Oxford University Press, 1957), and Herbert William Horwill, *A Dictionary of Modern American Usage* (*Ibid.*, 1935) are all helpful in the development of exactitude in language. Albert H. Marckwardt, *American English* (*Ibid.*, 1958) is a useful introduction. Bergen Evans and Cornelia Evans, *A Dictionary of Contemporary American Usage* (New York: Random House, c. 1957) offers a somewhat more flexible approach than do works that follow the lead of Fowler. Henry M. Silver, "Putting It on Paper," *PMLA*, LXV (Apr. 1950), 9-20, and *The New York Times Style Book* (New York 36: Dept. SB, New York Times, 1957; 102 pp. $1.00) are excellent on the preparation of manuscript for publication. For the way in which one especially felicitous writer developed his style see Charlotte Watkins Smith, "Carl Becker: The Historian as a Literary Craftsman," *William and Mary Quarterly*, Ser. III, Vol. IX (July 1952), 291-316, and her *Carl Becker: On History and the Climate of Opinion* (Ithaca: Cornell University Press. 1956: xi, 225 pp.).

for the baron or earl of Knightsbridge, with a "courtesy title" — Lord John Knight, borne by a younger son. (See Valentine Heywood, *British Titles* .... London: A. C. Black, c. 1953.)

    f. Numerals. In your text you should, as a rule, spell out numbers of one or two digits, but use numerals for those running to three or more. Also spell out a number at the beginning of a sentence and, in this case, all subsequent numbers in the sentence or following closely thereafter; or, preferably, contrive to begin the sentence with another word. In any form of tabulation or in groups containing numbers both over and under three digits, use Arabic numerals throughout. Centuries may be referred to either by numeral or in written form — 14th century or fourteenth century (sometimes capitalized, if one chooses, as 14th Century or Fourteenth Century) — so long as you are consistent.

    2. Learning by example. All thinking creatures learn by observation, imitation, experimentation, and constant practice. Cultivate a discriminating selectivity. Strive to improve your taste to the point where it automatically rejects the meretricious and banal. Turn to the vast treasure house of all past world literature for models to be found in both historical and imaginative writing. Remember the example of young Benjamin Franklin, forced to abandon the hope of grammar school and college, who found in the *Spectator* papers an example of urbane incisiveness (not unlike the style that characterizes today's *New Yorker* magazine) that helped him to develop one of the most effective writing styles in an age of literary elegance. Concentrate upon the writers who are best suited to point the way to your own fullest potentialities.

    3. Practice makes — . There is no substitute for writing and re-writing, for continually rising to the challenge of new undertakings. Get into the habit of writing, before the habit of not writing becomes fixed.

    Strive for consistent improvement. It often helps to come back, after an interval of time, to that which you have previously written so that you may read it with something of the critical eye of a stranger and thus more readily detect any weakness of thought or awkwardness of expression. You will gradually develop a trained eye and "inner ear" that will enable you to recognize, in rereading your successive drafts, "the one best way" to evolve and express your thought. There is drudgery in research and writing, as in any undertaking. But it is more than compensated for by those exhilarating periods, which will increase as you acquire a mastery of your field and a facility of expression, when the ideas and phrases flow easily from your mind and pen. Whatever the material compensation, the psychic rewards are beyond price. There is, above all, the satisfaction of coming to a better understanding of the world about you — and hence of yourself. Thus can you hope, both through the discovery of things previously unknown and in the manner in which you live, to make a contribution, however modest, to the truth that is history.

Courtesy of <i>The Washington Post and Times-Herald</i>
and permission of United Features Syndicate.